AS CHINA

ENGLAND.

Frontispiece. Eighteenth century pieces. Lowestoft tea bowl and saucer (16); Whieldon-type tea bowl and saucer (7); Lowestoft sucrier (20); Creamware jug (6); Worcester tea bowl (12); Caughley teapot (23); Derby cream boat (91).

Understanding
Miniature British Pottery and Porcelain
1730~Present Day

Maurice and Evelyn Milbourn

Antique Collectors' Club

First published 1983
© 1983 Maurice and Evelyn Milbourn
Reprinted 1995

World copyright reserved

ISBN 1 85149 237 2

British Library Cataloguing-in-Publication Data
A catalogue record for this book is available from the British Library

Printed in England on Consort Royal Satin paper
from Donside Mills, Aberdeen, by the
Antique Collectors' Club Ltd., Woodbridge, Suffolk IP12 1DS

Antique Collectors' Club

The Antique Collectors' Club was formed in 1966 and quickly grew to a five figure membership spread throughout the world. It publishes the only independently run monthly antiques magazine, *Antique Collecting*, which caters for those collectors who are interested in widening their knowledge of antiques, both by greater awareness of quality and by discussion of the factors which influence the price that is likely to be asked. The Antique Collectors' Club pioneered the provision of information on prices for collectors and the magazine still leads in the provision of detailed articles on a variety of subjects.

It was in response to the enormous demand for information on 'what to pay' that the price guide series was introduced in 1968 with the first edition of *The Price Guide to Antique Furniture* (completely revised 1978 and 1989), a book which broke new ground by illustrating the more common types of antique furniture, the sort that collectors could buy in shops and at auctions rather than the rare museum pieces which had previously been used (and still to a large extent are used) to make up the limited amount of illustrations in books published by commercial publishers. Many other price guides have followed, all copiously illustrated, and greatly appreciated by collectors for the valuable information they contain, quite apart from prices. The Price Guide Series heralded the publication of many standard works of reference on art and antiques. *The Dictionary of British Art* (now in six volumes), *The Pictorial Dictionary of British 19th Century Furniture Design, Oak Furniture* and *Early English Clocks* were followed by many deeply researched reference works such as *The Directory of Gold and Silversmiths,* providing new information. Many of these books are now accepted as the standard work of reference on their subject.

The Antique Collectors' Club has widened its list to include books on gardens and architecture. All the Club's publications are available through bookshops world-wide and a full catalogue of all these titles is available free of charge from the addresses below.

Club membership, open to all collectors, costs little. Members receive free of charge *Antique Collecting*, the Club's magazine (published ten times a year), which contains well-illustrated articles dealing with the practical aspects of collecting not normally dealt with by magazines. Prices, features of value, investment potential, fakes and forgeries are all given prominence in the magazine.

Among other facilities available to members are private buying and selling facilities, the longest list of 'For Sales' of any antiques magazine, an annual ceramics conference and the opportunity to meet other collectors at their local antique collectors' clubs. There are over eighty in Britain and more than a dozen overseas. Members may also buy the Club's publications at special pre-publication prices.

As its motto implies, the Club is an organisation designed to help collectors get the most out of their hobby: it is informal and friendly and gives enormous enjoyment to all concerned.

For Collectors —By Collectors —About Collecting

ANTIQUE COLLECTORS' CLUB
5 Church Street, Woodbridge, Suffolk IP12 1DS, UK
Tel: 01394 385501 Fax: 01394 384434
——— or ———
Market Street Industrial Park. Wappingers' Falls. NY 12590. USA

Contents

Colour Plates

Note: The bracketed numbers which appear in the captions to the Colour Plates refer to the Figure numbers of the relevant black and white illustrations.

Authors' note

We started collecting miniature pottery and porcelain in 1969 and quickly found it becoming an absorbing retirement hobby. However, the wide variety of potters making miniature wares in many different materials, shapes and styles, coupled with the small amount of published information, meant that the subject had to be studied in some depth. The results of that study, as presented herein, are no more than a preliminary assessment of miniature wares, brought together in the hope that it may be of interest to other collectors and perhaps form a foundation for further work.

Acknowledgements

The authors are indebted to many people for help and advice freely given, and received most gratefully. Thus, Messrs. Geoffrey Godden, Arnold Mountford and Henry Sandon have always been very helpful in attributing and dating specimens submitted to them, and we have benefited greatly from the experience of several knowledgeable dealers.

Miss M.E. Dickinson, whose family had lived at Bisham Abbey, Berkshire, kindly lent us her print of 'Bysham Monastery', which led to the fascinating hunt for the origins of other prints on the 'English Views' set. Much courteous help was received from the staff of the Reference Department of Birmingham Public Libraries in this hunt. To all of these we tender our most grateful thanks.

We are also indebted to the various organisations who have given courteous permission to use their photographs, and who are acknowledged on the illustrations. Unfortunately, the sizes of some pieces could no longer be traced.

All other illustrations are of items in our collection.

Chapter 1

An Introduction

Many kinds of small items can be the subjects of interest and of collections, such as miniature portraits, apprentice pieces in furniture, enamelled boxes, vinaigrettes or scent bottles. They attract by reason of their workmanship, skill or artistry, but their size is no minor cause of their appeal. Miniature pottery and porcelain are of the same nature, and pieces have been made as long as man has been baking clay.

Archaeological excavations in various parts of the world have found figurines of men and animals as well as small pots or other domestic articles. Their purpose may have been votive, for offerings to the gods, funerary, for use in the after-life, as playthings for children or even for the amusement of adults. The fashioning of small articles seems to have had a fascination for potters, and has persisted through the ages up to the present day, although it may have been obscured at times by commercial motives. In consequence, the field of miniature pottery and porcelain is as wide and as long as that of pottery and porcelain itself, and could not be adequately covered herein. A careful definition of the scope of this book is therefore needed.

We shall be dealing with small items, in pottery and porcelain, too large for the doll's house, mostly too small for ordinary use, made in this country between the middle of the eighteenth century and the present day. Specifically excluded are figures of persons and animals, commemoratives and crested wares, which have their own literature.

Our subject matter, then, includes teasets and dinner sets, children's plates, cradles, ewers and basins, jugs, mugs, jelly moulds, taper candlesticks and a few decorative items. This is the scope of the authors' collection which forms the backbone of this monograph, fleshed out and augmented with items from other sources.

The text will be mainly concerned with a description of the various items, but there are other more general objectives, viz:

(1) to provide guidance in dating

(2) to establish the general characteristics of miniature wares from the defined period

(3) to seek trends in shape, style or decoration

(4) to compare miniature with full-size pieces, and to define similarities and differences

(5) to promulgate observations on miniature wares that may be relevant to other pieces.

The choice of subject matter is determined largely by the authors' likes and by what is available. While a few special or rare pieces are included, most of the text is concerned with material that can still be found in shops, fairs and at auction, at prices that are not too excessive (although there have been considerable rises in prices over the past few years). It represents the ordinary run of production from various factories, known and unknown, rather than an esoteric museum collection. Attention is directed to products more than to manufacturers.

Literature on miniature wares is restricted to a chapter in one or two books, a few magazine articles and an occasional mention in books on pottery and porcelain. The most comprehensive is a chapter in Katharine Morrison McClinton's *Antiques in Miniature* (1970), which lists numerous items mostly in American collections and museums. However, it contains many doubtful attributions and statements, and is of no great use to British collectors. There is also a chapter in *Miniature Antiques* by Jean Latham (1972) but it deals only briefly with the sort of items discussed herein. Whiter's *Spode* (1970) contains outline drawings of many miniature wares taken from the 1820 Shape Book, and a photograph or two. His extracts from early account books also show that 'toys' were a commercial proposition, and not travellers' samples.

Lowestoft Porcelain in Norwich Castle Museum, Vol. 1, Blue and White by Sheena Smith (Norfolk Museums Service, 1975) has details of many miniature items including teapots, tea bowls, saucers, sucriers, cream jugs and coffee cups. The Norwich Castle Museum collection of Lowestoft porcelain is acknowledged to be the finest in public hands. 'Miniature Lowestoft China' an article by D.M. Hunting in the November-December 1949 issue of *The Antique Collector* is also worth studying, although superseded somewhat by the later publication.

Several books on pottery and porcelain have references to miniature wares and perhaps some illustrations. However, in none of them does this aspect form a substantial part of the text. They include *The Pottery and Porcelain of Swansea and Nantgarw* by E. Morton Nance (1942); *The Illustrated Guide to Staffordshire Salt-Glazed Stoneware* by A.R. Mountford (1971); *English Blue and White Porcelain of the 18th Century* by Bernard Watney (2nd Edition, 1973); *Caughley and Worcester Porcelains 1775-1800* by G.A. Godden (re-issued by the Antique Collectors' Club, 1981); *The Rockingham Pottery* by A.A. Eaglestone and T.A. Lockett (Municipal Museum and Art Gallery, Rotherham 1964); *Davenport Pottery and Porcelain* by T.A. Lockett (1972); and there are a few illustrations in *Illustrated Encyclopaedia of British Pottery and Porcelain* by G.A. Godden (1966).

Two further magazine articles, although brief, are useful and informative; 'Blues in Miniature by R.K. Henrywood (*Art and Antiques Weekly,* 24th August 1974) and 'Blue and White Miniature Porcelains' by Simon Spero (*Antique Dealer and Collectors' Guide,* March 1972). The latter ends with a relevant paragraph:

> Strangely enough, I am unable to end this brief article by recommending a book which deals with the subject in greater depth because there isn't one. Even the best books on English Porcelain do scant justice to this minor, but understandably popular, aspect of china collecting.

We adopt the usual definitions when speaking of pottery and porcelain, namely that porcelain is (almost always) translucent when held to an ordinary light bulb, and pottery is opaque. The former includes bone china and the various porcelain pastes used in the eighteenth century, while the latter covers earthenware and the various types of stoneware. Recognising that some pieces of pottery can show very slight translucency when held to an ordinary light bulb, tests have been made with a much more powerful light source by holding the item near the lens of a projector in a dark room. This procedure often reveals thin areas, and may also be indicative of firing temperature. The colour of the transmitted light is usually a deep brownish red, but it can be nearly white. It should be noted that many pottery items remain opaque even to this powerful light source.

The sonorous note emitted when a piece of porcelain is suitably supported and struck is well known, and there are occasional references in the literature to a similar ring from pieces of pottery. This sonority test has been used frequently on items in the authors' collection, and it, like the translucency test, is an indication of degree of compaction and hence of firing temperature. Measurements of density lead to the same end, and will be referred to occasionally.

The order of presentation of the material has been adopted to elucidate the objectives mentioned previously. Teaware is the most numerous, covers the whole period, and forms a good starting point. Items for coffee are also included, because combined tea and coffee services were often made.

Chapter 2
Teaware

When tea was first introduced to this country in the middle of the seventeenth century, it was sufficiently expensive to confine it to the wealthy, who, in any event, would use small teapots, probably imported from China. As the price fell, more and more potters made teapots and related items, until eventually miniature pieces appeared, described in potters' record books as 'toys'. These were certainly available in the 1740s and probably before (Figure 1).

The word 'toy' requires some discussion. In the eighteenth century it had several meanings, including (i) a child's plaything, (ii) a small item for the amusement or delectation of adults (as in 'Chelsea Toys') or, (iii) in combination, to indicate size. The first meaning has persisted and taken over, the second has practically disappeared, and the third survives in such expressions as 'toy dog', meaning a small breed. There is no certainty, then, that items described by potters as 'toys' were intended to be playthings, but doubtless many of them were so used. The description may have been no more than an indication of size, i.e. a piece much smaller

Figure 1. Astbury-type miniature teapot, brown and white, 3½ins.:88mm high, c.1740. City Museum and Art Gallery, Stoke-on-Trent.

than that in normal use. The earlier small teapots would not be called 'toys', because they were of the then normal size.

When the lady of the house gave a tea party, the children, particularly the girls, might have been allowed to participate. The desire to emulate their elders would stimulate a demand for miniature pieces, a demand that the potters would be only too glad to meet. Some pieces, then, would suffer in the nursery, but others were probably treasured in cabinets or on dressers or sideboards. That any have survived for more than two hundred years is remarkable.

Saltglaze Ware

The type of white pottery developed in the early years of the eighteenth century is usually known as Staffordshire saltglaze, although it was doubtless also made elsewhere. It is hardly ever marked, but many pieces demonstrate admirably the skill and artistry of the potter. Of the items in Figure 2, the teapot is some 2ins.:52mm high and the little bowl no more than ½in.:13mm. The cup has a delightful shape, and the saucer's delicate pattern shows how well the technique of salt glazing is suited to moulding. When allied with slip casting (Figure 3) the result is a triumph not only for the potter but also for the mould maker. This teapot, at 4ins.:102mm high, is perhaps on the large side to be regarded as a miniature, but it is smaller than many. Both it and the items in the previous figure were made in the mid-1740s. A plate (Figure 4)

Figure 2. Saltglaze cup and saucer, bowl and teapot, teapot 2ins.:52mm high, c.1745. Sotheby's.

Figure 3. Saltglaze teapot and cover 4ins.:102mm high, c.1745. Sotheby's.

Figure 4. Saltglaze plate 4½ins.:116mm diameter, c.1760.

decorated only with a typical crisply moulded border and a wavy edge is also on the large side, while being smaller than most. The fact that the plate warped in the kiln demonstrates one of the problems faced by eighteenth century potters in trying to control their manufacturing conditions by rule of thumb. Although saltglaze is hard fired, the plate has no sonority when suitably supported and lightly struck. There are no obvious defects, but they may have been carefully concealed in repair. This item was probably made in about 1760.

Decoration of saltglaze with enamel colours is seen in the charming little teapot in Figure 5, which has flowers and leaves in red, yellow and green on a black background. It is dated c.1755.

Figure 5. Saltglaze teapot enamelled in red, yellow and green on a black ground 2½ins.:63mm high, c.1755. City Museum and Art Gallery, Stoke-on-Trent.

Figure 6. Creamware tea bowl, saucer and jug. Jug 2ins.:52mm high. 1760-1770.

Creamware

The delightful tea bowl, saucer and jug in Figure 6 are all in the same medium shade of creamware decorated only with beading on the edges of the tea bowl and jug and in the well of the saucer. Their similarities tend to foster the belief that they are parts of the same toy teaset, although they were purchased as separate items. The jug and bowl were thrown and all three finished with a smooth yellowish glaze, showing some crazing on the bowl. The inside of the jug is not completely glazed. Note the delicate and stylish strap handle, pinched at its lower end. Items of this type are so often described as Leeds that one hesitates to use the term again, but the signs point in this direction and to a date c.1760-70. The main attribute of these three pieces is their superb potting; the jug, 2ins.:52mm high, weighs only 20 grams, i.e. about ⅔ of an ounce. It is also worth noting that the saucer has a reasonably sonorous ring.

The Whieldon-type tea bowl and saucer illustrated in Figure 7 are of a similar standard of excellence. The body is creamware and the glaze is streaked with manganese brown, and is crazed. In particular, the tea bowl, ¹³/₁₆ in.:21mm high, is most delicately potted with a slightly everted rim and a neat little foot rim.

Further Whieldon-type items illustrated in Figure 8 show very well the general shapes of many eighteenth century wares, a

Colour Plate 1. Items decorated with high temperature colours. Plate (219); Tureen and stand (125); Cradle (182).

Figure 7. Whieldon-type tea bowl and saucer. Saucer 3¼ins.:80mm diameter. 1760-1770.

Figure 8. Whieldon-type toy teawares. Teapot 2½ins.:64mm. 1760-70.
Sotheby's.

globular teapot, a simple circular sucrier, a deep saucer with a tea bowl and a milk jug with a pinched-in lip. The other item could well be a teapot stand. All are also from the 1760-70 period.

Photographs cannot do justice to the merits of these creamware items. They need to be handled to appreciate the delicacy of their potting and the quality of their glaze.

Tin-Glazed Earthenware

The only tin-glazed items of miniature teaware known to the authors are illustrated in *Pottery and Porcelain Tablewares* by John P. Cushion (1976), p. 73. They include a teapot, jug, tea bowls and saucers decorated in high temperature blue, reputedly made in Liverpool c.1760. They give the impression of being made in a material most unsuitable for teaware, particularly the edges of

Figure 9. Teaware, painted blue decoration on white slip. Teapot 3³/₁₆ins.:81mm high. Possibly Liverpool, c.1790.

the bowls where the glaze has cracked away.

A development from tin-glazed ware was to cover an earthenware body with a white slip, decorated and finished with a clear glaze. Such material is illustrated in Figure 9 including a globular teapot, 3³/₁₆ins.:81mm high, and sugar box, both having typical late eighteenth century shapes. The underglaze blue painted decoration in the Chinese style has been completed with a minimum of brush strokes, and here and there has run in the glaze. The body is of a pale brown biscuit colour, and the glaze has a blue tint and is crazed. There is no breaking away of the glaze and slip at the edges, making this a more satisfactory body for teaware than tin-glazed earthenware. These items are tentatively ascribed to Liverpool, c.1790.

Eighteenth Century Porcelain Teaware

Manufacture of porcelain in this country did not start until the middle of the eighteenth century, with Chelsea in about 1745, quickly followed by Bow, Bristol, Derby, Worcester, Liverpool and Lowestoft, and later by Plymouth and Caughley. The general characteristics of their wares are well documented (e.g. *Guide to English Porcelain* by Geoffrey Godden, 1978, and many specialist books) but there is little information regarding miniature wares.

Teawares in 'toy' sizes were made by Bow, Worcester, Liverpool, Lowestoft and Caughley and perhaps at other factories. They were mostly in blue and white, painted or printed, but some polychrome enamelled items were produced for instance at Lowestoft during its later years. Teapots are usually globular, tea bowls are unhandled, but coffee cups have handles. Saucers may be deep or shallow, foot rims are common, but there is usually no well in the upper surface. Sizes are not standardised, and small variations are likely to be encountered; this is most noticeable in Caughley wares because they are the commonest.

Figure 10. Worcester coffee cup and saucer, mid-1750. Sotheby's.

Figure 11. Worcester teapot 3¼ins.:82mm high, c.1760-65. Sotheby's.

Figure 12. Worcester tea bowl and saucer. Saucer 4ins.:103mm diameter.

An early Worcester coffee cup and saucer painted in blue with foliage, a bird on a rock and a fence are illustrated in Figure 10. They are fine examples of Worcester products in the mid-1750s; note the very slightly everted rim of the cup, a characteristic that persisted for many years.

The quality of the teapot in Figure 11 is apparent in its fine body, its elegant but very practical shape and its restrained decoration. It is some 3¼ins.:82mm high and was made at Worcester in about 1760-65.

The tea bowl and saucer in Figure 12 are included as examples of Worcester products printed in underglaze blue. They are decorated

Figure 13. Bow miniature tea bowls, saucers and sucrier, c. 1760. Sotheby's.

Figure 14. Bow miniature tête-à-tête,c.1760. Sotheby's.

with the well-known 'Three Flowers' pattern taken from a copper plate engraved with thick, heavy lines. They are a handsome pair, but the saucer, 4½ins.:114mm in diameter, may be a little large for the bowl, which is 1⅜ins.:35mm high. They date from c.1780.

The most frequently encountered pattern on Bow miniatures is one of grapes and vine leaves painted in underglaze blue (Figure 13). These items were made in about 1760, as also were those in Figure 14, described as part of a tête-à-tête and decorated in enamels. In general, one expects Bow pieces to be rather heavily potted, apparent in the handle of the teapot. The shape and position of this handle are worth noting — its small size and its

Figure 15. Lowestoft blue-painted teaware. Teapot 2⅞ins.:73mm high.
Norfolk Museums Service, (Norwich Castle Museum).

lower end terminating at the greatest diameter of the body. It may also be noted that the two sucriers are different in shape, in the top rim of the body and the means for lifting the cover.

The Lowestoft factory's output of miniature wares was of fair proportions, remembering that it relied mainly on local trade. Items decorated in painted underglaze blue with the pattern known as 'Chinese River Scene' are illustrated in Figure 15. They are from the 1760-65 period, the teapot being 2⅞ ins.:73mm high overall. A later pattern from 1770-80 and known as 'Chinese Garden Scene' is on the tea bowl and saucer in Figure 16. The potting is good, the decoration naïve but neatly executed and the glaze adequate but rather soft. Both these blue and white patterns seem to be restricted to miniature wares, and form a useful means of identifying some unmarked Lowestoft production.

Figure 16. Lowestoft tea bowl and saucer, blue painted. Saucer 2⅞ins.:73mm diameter. 1770-80.

Figure 17. Lowestoft teapot and cover, blue painted, 4³/₁₆ ins.:106mm high. 1770-80. Sotheby's.

Figure 18. Lowestoft teapot and cover, blue printed, 4³/₁₆ins.:106mm high. 1770-80. Sotheby's.

Two other teapots in underglaze blue from 1770-80 period are illustrated in Figures 17 and 18. The former has a painted pattern but the latter carries one that is printed, and is usually called the 'Good Cross Chapel' design. Both are about 4¼ins.:106mm high, and points worth noting are the slightly curved spouts, the plain loop handles and the simple finials.

Polychrome decoration was used at Lowestoft in its later years, 1780-1800, some miniature examples being shown in Figure 19. The saucer is in pink, purple, green and black, which are also used on the plain tea bowl with the addition of brick red, while on the ribbed tea bowl purple is replaced by underglaze blue. A sucrier of

Figure 19. Lowestoft polychrome tea bowls and saucer. Saucer 3ins.:76mm diameter, c.1780-1800. Norfolk Museums Service (Norwich Castle Museum).

Figure 20. Lowestoft polychrome sucrier (lid missing), 2ins.:50mm high. 1780-1800.

which the lid is missing (Figure 20) is decorated in pink, green and black for the little sprigs and the border, while the continuous wavy lines are in brown. It is a charming piece, with a clear white body and wet-looking enamels, the potting being on the heavy side.

A few miniature items were made at some of the Liverpool factories, and the teapot in Figure 21 must be regarded as a rarity. It is some 3½ins.:88mm high, decorated in underglaze blue with a country scene and ascribed to the William Reid factory.

More miniature porcelain items were produced at the Caughley factory than at any other eighteenth century concern, or, at least, more have survived. They are from the 1780-90 period and are

Figure 21. William Reid teapot and cover 3½ins.:88mm high, 1755-61. Sotheby's.

Figure 22. Caughley coffee pot (lid missing) cup and saucer. Blue painted, coffee pot 2¹⁵/₁₆ ins.:74mm high, 1780-90.

decorated with either of two patterns, one painted and one printed, both in underglaze blue. In general they are well potted in a soap-stone body similar to that used at Worcester, and have a most attractive simplicity. The painted pattern is the commoner, and has a tree in the centre of an island, with a small building at each end. The sun as well as some birds and boats are often included. It is illustrated in Figures 22 and 23, the former showing a coffee pot (lid missing) and coffee cup and saucer, and the latter a teapot, sucrier, tea bowl and saucer and plate. The coffee pot is 2¹⁵/₁₆ ins.:74mm high and the teapot 3¼ins.:83mm. The printed pattern is a reduced version of the well-known 'Fisherman', 'Cormorant' or 'Pleasure Boat' pattern shown on a tea bowl and saucer and jug in Figure 24. The jug is 1⅞ins.:47mm high.

These eighteenth century wares, both pottery and porcelain, are the cream of miniature teaware, and one has to remember that cream is more expensive than milk. Their chief attribute is their individuality, in that they show signs of the skill and artistry that went into making them. With the pottery items it is virtually impossible to assign them to a manufacturer, but it is easier with porcelain, probably because of the amount of research that has gone into this area. It seems apparent that manufacturers did not try specifically to appeal to children. Decoration if present is simple but not childish.

Colour Plate 2. Porcelain items with enamel decoration. Cake plate (64); Worcester coffee pot (26); Cup (59); Minton cake plate (74); Teapot (67); Cup (43).

Figure 23. Caughley teaware, blue painted, Teapot 3¼ins.:82mm high. 1780-90.

Figure 24. Caughley tea bowl, saucer and jug, blue printed. Jug 1⅞ins.:48mm high. 1780-90.

Nineteenth Century Wares

Bone china has been the standard English porcelain body since it was first introduced, possibly by Spode, in about 1800. It rapidly replaced all the various porcelain mixes, hard and soft pastes, steatitic and phosphatic compositions, used by the various factories up to that time. Worcester retained their well-tried and popular steatite mix until about 1830, but they were the last to change.

With pottery there was less standardisation, but, with the exception of coloured bodies, the aim was to produce a white surface which could be decorated with print or paint, and given a lustrous glaze. Several varieties of stone china were introduced, each with its fancy name; Mason's 'Ironstone China' is the best known. It seems that each manufacturer had his own pet formula, the object being to produce items that were stronger than plain earthenware, and perhaps to impress the public.

The degree of standardisation that came with the nineteenth century arose, of course, from the Industrial Revolution, and we shall be watching the effect of this upheaval upon quality of product — the ordinary product made for sale and not the product made for prestige. At the same time, standardisation brought pottery and porcelain closer together, so that there is no need to study them separately. In fact, many manufacturers, particularly the larger, more influential ones, made both simultaneously.

(i) Early Years (1800-30)

Two tea bowls and saucers in porcelain enamelled with flowers and sprigs and simple borders, are from about 1800 (Figure 25). The two saucers, 4⁵⁄₁₆ ins.:110mm in diameter, are almost identical in size and shape, but the tea bowls are different, as are also the palettes and styles of decoration. The one has pink, green, purple, maroon and blue, and the other pink, green and purple. Note also the double row of blue dots surrounding the larger flowers on the first. This has the number 873 enamelled in red and the other 878 in green. They probably come from different, unknown, factories, and are a little on the large size for miniatures. Nevertheless they are charming pieces.

Even if they were not marked, one could perhaps have guessed that the coffee pot, teacup and saucer in Figure 26 were Worcester

Colour Plate 3. Painted pottery items. Spode dish (as 28); Tinglaze vase (226); Wemyss plate (220); Wedgwood plate (95); Teapot (36); Peafowl sucrier (41).

Figure 25. Porcelain tea bowls and saucers, enamelled in Polychrome. Saucers 4⁵/₁₆ ins.:110mm diameter, c.1800.

Figure 26. Worcester coffee pot, cup and saucer. Pot 4⁹/₁₆ ins.:116mm high, c.1805.

33

Figure 27. Pottery jug and tea bowl. Jug 3ins.:75mm high, c.1805.

from the delightful simple decoration in gilding and maroon. As it is, the coffee pot and cup have an incised B, and the saucer is impressed BFB under a crown. They are all therefore from the Worcester factory a few years after the turn of the century. The coffee pot was thrown and is very well potted, it has a delicate handle and only one largish hole at the base of the spout. The cup and deep saucer seem to belong to each other, but the former was probably intended for tea rather than coffee. All three pieces have the excellent finish one expects from Worcester, but the saucer has been broken into two and mended.

Chinoiserie patterns have been noted on eighteenth century porcelain and a further example is illustrated on the pottery jug and tea bowls in Figure 27. This pattern, called 'Curling Palm Tree' is known to have been used by Job Ridgway in about 1805, but it is possibly unwise to make a firm ascription on the basis of pattern alone. This is in underglaze blue with the usual selection of pagodas, steps, bridges, buildings, foliage, flowers and occasional figures. So far as one can see from rather blurred prints, the engraving is entirely line. The glaze is distinctly blue, but quite lustrous.

Six of the exhibits at the Spode Bicentenary Exhibition at the Royal Academy in 1970 were of Toy Teaware, and one is illustrated here as Figure 28. It comprises a ball-shaped teapot and two Bute-shaped cups and saucers, the cups having typical Spode handles. They are in pottery, beautifully light in weight, and very well

Figure 28. Spode pottery teapot, cups and saucers.
Teapot 2¾ins.:70mm high, c.1814.

potted. The decoration is firstly a pale blue underglaze ground, with flowers and foliage in brown, pink and occasional turquoise, all overglaze. It extends right down the inside walls of the cups. The teapot has six strainer holes at the base of the spout, and the steam hole in the lid is drilled through the finial. The pattern number is 2284, first introduced in about 1814.

Some later Spode items include drabware cup, saucer and cream jug decorated only with broad lines of gilding (Figure 29). The interiors of cup and jug are covered with white slip. They are well

Figure 29. Spode pottery drabware cup, saucer and jug. Jug
2⁷/₁₆ins.:62mm high. 1825-30.

Figure 30. Spode pottery green printed cup and saucer. Saucer 4½ins.:114mm diameter, c.1830.

potted, but the body seems to be heavy. Only the saucer is marked, impressed SPODE, the date being perhaps 1825-30. The cream jug is of the shape to go with the teapot in the previous figure, but the cup is now London shape, as also are the cup and saucer in Figure 30. These are decorated with a green underglaze print of a trellis pattern, and both have a printed SPODE mark. They were made in about 1830 or shortly thereafter. We have seen a badly damaged ball-shaped teapot with this green pattern.

The 'London' shape of teapot (Figure 31) is not particularly common among Spode wares. This example has 'Milkmaid' pattern and its usual border in underglaze blue, and a printed SPODE mark. Its standards of potting and decoration are rather

Figure 31. Spode pottery teapot. Milkmaid pattern. 5⅞ins.:150mm long. 1825-30.

Figure 32. Pottery teaware blue and white, Broseley print. Teapot 3⁷/₁₆ ins.:87mm high. 1815-25.

lower than those of the other excellent Spode pieces described here, and it is difficult to date, but it might be 1825-30.

This London shape seems to have been popular in the 1820s; in fact, one unidentified manufacturer made at least four examples in pottery illustrated here with associated wares. The first (Figure 32) is decorated with an underglaze blue Broseley pattern on a white body and includes teapot, sugar box, creamer and cups and saucers. The cups are Bute-shaped. A set in buff-coloured pottery is decorated with black overglaze prints of Adam Buck type subjects, four in all, and includes teapot, creamer, sugar box, bowl and cups and saucers (Figure 33). Three shapes of cup are shown in Figure 34, all with the same two black overglaze prints, one on each side. Another buff-based set (Figure 35) decorated with the same four subjects similarly distributed but in overglaze sepia, comprises teapot, bowl and cups and saucers. While the same set of engravings was used for the black prints a different set produced the sepia decoration. Finally, a teapot with no other pieces (Figure 36) has a white body painted overglaze with pink flowers and brown leaves.

Figure 33. Pottery teaware, black and buff, Adam Buck style prints, teapot 3⁷/₁₆ ins.:87mm high, 1815-25.

Figure 34. Three cups, black and buff, Adam Buck style print. 1½ — 1¹⁵/₁₆ ins.:38-46mm high. 1815-25.

Figure 35. Pottery teaware, sepia and buff, Adam Buck style prints, teapot 3⁷/₁₆ ins.:87mm high, 1815-25.

Figure 36. Pottery teapot. Brown and pink enamelled on white. 3⁷/₁₆ ins.:87mm high. 1815-25.

The four teapots (32, 33, 35 and 36) are sufficiently similar in size and shape to have come from the same mould, and their handles, lids, finials and spouts are identical, as well as the six strainer holes at the base of the spout. The two sugar boxes and the two creamers are also of the same size and shape, but there are five shapes of cups and saucers and two of slop bowls. Nevertheless, the evidence is very strong that all pieces came from the same factory, which must have had a prolific output of miniature wares for so many to have survived. The items are of good quality, well potted, decorated and glazed, the last being bluish on the white body and

Figure 37. Pottery teaware, black print. Teapot 3⁹/₁₆ ins.:91mm high. 1820-30.

yellowish on the buff. They were probably made about 1815-25, and one would hazard a guess that the painted teapot was the earliest, followed by the blue-on-white, the black-on-buff and finally the sepia. Those saucers that are not crazed or cracked have some sonority. There is little translucency to a powerful light source, except with the blue-on-white teapot, which shows much. Rippling of the glaze is common.

The teapot, creamer and sugar box in Figure 37 appear to be similar to those just discussed, but there are differences in the sizes and shapes of the lids, the position of the knobs on the inside of the handles, and the number of strainer holes, eighteen in this case. They are in white pottery, decorated overglaze with a black print of a basket of flowers, and finished with a near colourless glaze. They are marked with an impressed heart, but it seems that they are not of Swansea manufacture. They are probably from the 1820 period.

Continuing with the same theme and in the same period, a charming example of London shape (Figure 38) is decorated with pink lustre, some painted, some applied with a sponge or even a loofah. The scene is a simple house and garden, neatly painted, and clearer than many such lustre items. The shapes of handle and spout are attractive, but the finial is not the original. This pottery item may have originated in the North East, but it is by no means certain.

The more usual type of pink lustre decoration is illustrated in Figure 39 on pottery cup, saucer and plate. The painting is crude and elementary, possibly done by children, but it has its own charm. The three items are well potted, and the saucer in particular has a good sonorous ring. They are rather later than the previous item, say 1830-40, but their point of origin is no more certain.

Figure 38. Pottery teapot pink lustre decoration, 3⁷/₁₆ ins.:87mm high. 1820-30.

Figure 39. Pottery cup, saucer and plate. Pink lustre cottage. Plate 5³/₁₆ ins.:132mm diameter. 1830-40.

Colour Plate 4. Items with lustre decoration. Silver resist saucer (40); Purple lustre teapot (38); Tureen with silver lustre (148); Jug with copper lustre (192).

Figure 40. Pottery tea bowl and saucer, silver resist lustre. Saucer 4⁵/₁₆ ins.:110mm diameter. 1820-25.

Silver resist lustre as well as ruby lustre was made in miniature size, the tea bowl and saucer in Figure 40 being decorated with the well-known resist pattern of grapes, vine leaves and tendrils on a white ground. They are well decorated as well as being well and lightly potted, and are good examples of their type, possibly 1820-25.

So called 'Peafowl' decoration (Figure 41) is most colourfully attractive, comprising a bird enamelled in pink, blue and yellow in a black outline, sitting on a branch among sponged green foliage. The teapot and sugar box have unusual shapes and appear to have been thrown rather than moulded. The steam hole is drilled through the finial, and the lids have been potted almost to a feather edge. One would call the decoration elementary but not crude. Dating is difficult but a combination of underglaze green and rippled glaze, particularly on the plate, might indicate 1825-30. McClinton illustrates very similar pieces, ascribing them to an unrecorded manufacturer G. Adams and Son, mid-nineteenth century.

Figure 41. Pottery teaware, Peafowl decoration. Teapot 2⅝ins.:66mm high. 1825-30.

Figure 42. Rogers pottery plate, Broseley blue print 3¹⁵/₁₆ ins.:100mm diameter, c.1820.

An interesting plate (that could be from either a tea or dinner set) is illustrated in Figure 42. It is printed in a pale underglaze blue with a Broseley pattern having only one man on the bridge walking away from the Pagoda. The two marks are ROGERS impressed and Semi-China in a square set on one corner, printed in underglaze blue. It is pleasant to be able at last to ascribe a piece to a manufacturer and to date it as c.1820.

So many unmarked items are described as Coalport that suspicions are naturally aroused. In the case of the two cups and saucers in Figure 43, the answer is either 'Maybe' or 'No', the latter being the more likely. They are in a fine white bone china with a slightly pinkish translucency, very well decorated with enamelled flower and foliage sprays in polychrome. These are excellent pieces, but the fact that they are not marked does not detract from — or add to — their intrinsic quality. However, their value would be increased if they had a well-known manufacturer's mark because either it helps to maintain their saleable value, or because the purchaser does not trust his own judgement and hopes to buy quality by name. This is much more apparent in the picture market, where provenance, signature and artist count so much. Returning to our cups and saucers, there are four different sprays, one each on the saucers and two on each cup. We date them tentatively to about 1830, but they could be later. The complete set would look magnificent.

The two cups in Figure 44 are also difficult to date, although their shape might indicate c.1825 (other pieces, discussed later,

Figure 43. Porcelain cups and saucers, enamelled with flower sprays. Saucers 4¹/₁₆ ins.:103mm diameter, c.1830.

Figure 44. Pottery cups, pencilled in maroon, overglaze. 1¼ins.:32mm high, c.1825.

indicate that dating on shape alone can be misleading). The cups are in pottery, tastefully pencilled inside and out in maroon. The imitation rivets on the handles add an interesting touch.

This discussion of miniature teaware produced during the early years of the nineteenth century indicates that many were attractive, some were beautiful and that most were interesting. There was less individuality than in the eighteenth century, probably due to standardisation and changes in manufacturing conditions, but potters apparently tried to maintain the standards of quality set by their predecessors.

(ii) Middle Period (1830-65)

As the century progressed, more and more people had incomes, from industry, commerce or trade, sufficiently large to enable them to buy variously priced presents for their children. Pottery and porcelain teasets would doubtless be intended for the girls, and it is surprising that so many were made and have survived, because girls were of no great account in the Victorian hierarchy. When searching *The Dictionary of National Biography* for the likely recipient of a set with the monogram FFL, we found that sons were listed by name but the total number of daughters only was recorded. But perhaps their fathers doted on them!

During this period also there were several changes in shapes and fashions; we shall endeavour to follow these in relation to miniature teawares.

*Figure 45. Pottery teaware, pale blue body with green underglaze print.
Teapot 4⁵/₁₆ ins.:110mm high. 1830-40.*

Developments from the London shape of teapot began to appear
in the early 1830s (Figure 45). The teapot, sugar box and cup and
saucer are in a pale blue pottery body with an underglaze green
print of a landscape with trees and flowers, an urn and a beehive.
The border is also floral; the finials and handles on the sugar box
are convolvulus flowers with a few moulded leaves, and the strainer
is a neatly drilled hemisphere. There is some moulding on body and
foot rim of teapot and sugar box, and on the teapot handle. The
pale blue base is like that produced by William Ridgway in the
1830-40 period, but there is no record that this was decorated with a
print. However, Coysh and Henrywood (*Dictionary of Blue and
White Printed Pottery,* Antique Collectors' Club, 1982) ascribe the
pattern, which they call 'Beehive', to William Ridgway also,
making this a positive attribution! These pieces are made and
decorated beautifully, and excellently glazed, but the combination
of green and blue has hardly come off.

Another pottery teapot, shown in Figure 46, is a more distant variation on the London shape, with an underglaze purple print of a log cabin with a simple star border. The border on the lid is different, but of the same colour; the lid must have been made to fit the teapot, because it is an excellent fit although needing to be curved in all three directions. The same standard of workmanship is shown in the potting of the body; although this must have been moulded, there is no evidence on the surface of mould joins. It is not easy to date, but 1835-40 may be appropriate.

The Godwins, Benjamin and John and Robert, were among the more prolific makers of miniature tewares in pottery, and for-

Figure 46. Pottery teapot, purple underglaze print. 4⅞ ins.:112mm high. 1835-40.

Figure 47. Benjamin Godwin pottery teaware. Underglaze green print. 'Caledonia'. Teapot 4⁵/₁₆ ins.:109mm high. 1835-40.

tunately marked many of their products. Godden (*Encyclopaedia of British Pottery and Porcelain Marks,* p. 277) notes that 'Many child's toy services bear BG marks'. The teaset illustrated in Figure 47 has the printed mark 'Caledonia BG' in a cartouche, and was made by Benjamin Godwin, 1834-41. It is decorated with a crisp underglaze green print of kilted horsemen in a highland landscape with an arcaded border having alternate vignettes of a dog and a fanciful bird. The potting is rather heavy and the ornate handle almost overpowers the teapot. The influence of the London shape is still discernible. Plate, cup and saucer are all acceptable; note particularly the shape of the cup and its handle.

Figure 48. 'Cottage' teaware. Underglaze brown print. Probably Godwin. Teapot 3⁷/₁₆ ins.:87mm high, c.1835.

The items in Figure 48 are informative as well as pleasant. The print is underglaze brown, indicating a date probably after 1830, but the shapes of teapot, sugar box and creamer, similar to those in Figure 33, would suggest something earlier. It seems that many shapes lasted for a considerable time, as long as they were saleable, in fact. The scene of a chalet in a wood is very similar to that in Figure 62 of *Blue-Printed Earthenware 1800-1850* by A.W. Coysh

(1972), even to the border and the vignettes therein. There must be some differences because the miniature saucer is 4⅜ins.:112mm in diameter and the Coysh plate 8½ins.:216mm. The latter is marked SWISS COTTAGE on a scroll above an 'M' in script , and is of Minton manufacture, whereas the miniature items are marked COTTAGE in an arc below 'G', and cannot be ascribed to Minton. Coysh notes that the Minton 'Genevese' pattern was also used by other potters, Thomas and Benjamin Godwin, for example, so the G could well refer to one of the Godwins. The similar shapes of 'Caledonia' and 'Cottage' cups and their handles point to Benjamin Godwin, who may have inherited them from his predecessors, Thomas and Benjamin. There is a different scene on the other side of all items except saucers, showing two fishermen in the foreground, a barge on the river, and a farm on the far bank.

The underglaze green pattern in Figure 49 is also by Benjamin Godwin, marked 'Peacock BG'. The transfer is crisp, particularly the extensive border, the cup handle is neat, but the potting is on the heavy side.

The partnership of John and Robert Godwin also started in 1834, but continued to 1866, and the wares to be discussed could

Figure 49. Benjamin Godwin pottery teaware. Underglaze green print 'Peacock'. Saucer 4¹/₁₆ ins.:113mm diameter, c.1840.

have been produced at any time during this period. The first (Figure 50) appears to be earlier rather than later, because the cup handle and the waisted cup resemble closely the same features on the 'Peacock' cup (Figure 49). The handle on the creamer is also very similar to that on the 'Caledonia' teapot (Figure 47). The well-transferred print in underglaze green is of a girl picking grapes as large as apricots from a vine taller than she. The wide border incorporates fanciful birds and flower sprays, and both print and border leave considerable areas of white china. A ring of moulded beads outlines the edge of the well in the saucer. The printed mark is a spray of vine leaves incorporating the words 'Fruit Girl' and the initials J. & R.G. Such pieces as remain of this set give a good impression.

The teacup and saucer in Figure 51 repeat the handle, waisted body and moulded beading noted on 'Fruit Girl', although sizes are slightly different. The print, again in underglaze green, shows a girl and a boy, both of whom appear to be left-handed, playing an esoteric game in a country house estate. The mark is a cartouche surrounding the title 'Juvenile Sports' and having the initials J. & R.G.

Figure 50. J & R Godwin pottery teaware. Underglaze green print 'Fruit Girl'. Plate 5¹/₈ ins.:130mm diameter, c.1845.

51

Figure 51. J & R. Godwin pottery cup and saucer. Underglaze green print 'Juvenile Sports'. 4⁷/₁₆ ins. :113mm diameter, c.1845.

The teapot and sugar box in Figure 52 have a round shape instead of the generally oval section that had persisted for many years. By comparison with other manufacturers (see page 56) this would indicate a date of about 1850. They are decorated with a print, in a heavy underglaze brown, of a girl kneeling beside a goat in front of a cottage. The border has C-scrolls between vignettes of mare and foal, cow and calf and sheep. This also is marked J. & R.G., with the name of the pattern 'GOAT' in a simple cartouche of C-scrolls.

Figure 52. J & R Godwin pottery teaware. Underglaze brown print 'Goat'. Teapot 3¹⁵/₁₆ ins.:100mm high at handle, c.1850.

A few general comments may be made on the Godwin wares. The quality is not particularly good, but potting, decoration and finish are of a reasonable standard. Some of the shapes do not appeal to modern eyes, but were doubtless acceptable to their contemporaries. The prints are apposite for small wares intended for children, and were probably restricted to this use. Many plates and saucers have a sonorous ring, except those that are crazed or cracked, and highly translucent areas are found on the 'Goat' teapot, sucrier and creamer and on the 'Caledonia' teapot. These are thin places and incipient potting faults, but several slightly translucent areas are found on other items.

There is a charming print of a boy pushing a wheelbarrow in which a girl is sitting, that occurs on both tea and dinner wares. An example in blue on a cup is shown in Figure 53. The other side of the cup has a blurred print of two children, probably a boy and a girl, sitting in a garden with a mansion in the background. The

Figure 53. Pottery cup. Underglaze blue print 'Wheelbarrow'. 1¾ins. :45mm high. 1840-45.

Figure 54. Copeland and Garrett pottery teapot and sucrier. Teapot 2¹¹/₁₆ ins.:68mm high, c.1835-40.

maker is not known, but the date might possibly be 1840-45. Further discussion will be found under 'Dinnerware'.

Copeland and Garrett succeeded Spode in 1833 but the teapot (Figure 54) made by the former is little different in shape from that made by Spode in 1814 (Figure 28). Similarly, the accompanying sugar box is of the shape that matches the teapot. These two items might be as late as 1840, demonstrating once again the remarkable longevity of some shapes. They have an underglaze green sheet pattern of stems and leaves with painted blue, pink and green additions that appear also to be underglaze. The teapot has a printed mark 'Copeland and Garrett late Spode, New Fayence' and the sugar box 'Copeland and Garrett New Blanche', surmounted by a crown. Both have a painted number 173. To us, they are interesting rather than beautiful, but they are light in weight.

A set of undoubted quality and most unusual shapes (Figure 55) has presented a problem that we may have resolved falsely. The various items are well and thinly potted with indented edges to cups and saucers, plates and bowl. The shapes of teapot and sugar box can be judged from the figure, but it is not immediately apparent that they are ten-sided. The fine white body is sparsely decorated in green underglaze, with a sheet pattern of tendrils and foliage, delicately enhanced with touches of blue, yellow and maroon over-

Figure 55. Pottery teaset, underglaze green print and enamels. Teapot 3¾ins.:95mm high, c.1840.

glaze. All cups and the bowl are fully decorated inside and out. The overall impression is of good design, manufacture and finishing in a first-class factory. The plates only have an impressed mark of 'Improved Stone China' in a double rectangle with random marks between the two lines. This mark is usually ascribed to the Meigh family and apparently persisted through three partnerships. However, we have seen an Amherst Japan plate with the standard Minton scroll mark in underglaze blue and number in red, with this impressed mark in addition. It may not be significant, but the lettering in the Meigh mark as shown in Godden's *Encyclopaedia* is in capitals, whereas that on the set being discussed has initial letters only in capitals and the remainder in neat lower-case. The problem then is one of ascription and the choice has been Minton. This makes dating no more precise than towards or about the middle of the century. The set is complete, apart from the creamer, there being teapot, sugar box, six cups and saucers, two plates and a slop bowl.

The two items in Figure 56 are both printed in strawberry pink although they appear to be otherwise unrelated. The deep saucer has a scene of a girl telling the fortunes of two serving maids at the back door, and is marked 'GIPSEY'; the plate with the lady riding side-saddle has a large mark with 'THOMPSON AND CO.' on a

Figure 56. Two pottery items. Underglaze pink prints. Saucer 4⁵/₁₆ ins.:110mm diameter, mid-19th century.

ribbon surmounted by a dove of peace, with 'GENUINE OPAQUE CHINA' below, the whole supported by two leafy branches. This company is not recorded, but it might refer to J. Thompson of the Hartshorne Pottery, Derbyshire. Both items are probably mid-century.

The set in Figure 57 provides a useful standard from which others can be dated approximately. Several of its pieces have the impressed mark of DAVENPORT in an arc over an anchor, with a number on each side of the stem of the anchor. Thus the 4 and 8 on the plates indicate that they were potted in 1848; similarly, the tea-pot and saucers were made in 1852. The cups, bowl and creamer have no impressed mark and that on the sugar box is indecipherable. Assuming that all items were decorated at the same time (which is likely) the plates were kept in store for four years between potting and painting. So what is the date of manufacture? One can only compromise and call it about 1850. However, the shapes are typical of products from a reasonably wide period about 1850. The painted overglaze decoration includes large pink lustre flowers with green and chocolate brown sprays and lustre flecks. The pink lustre flowers are so thin that loving care has washed many of them off. The pattern number 701 is painted in lustre on all items.

Figure 57. Davenport pottery teaware. Pink lustre & enamels. Teapot 4³/₁₆ ins.:106mm high at handle, c.1850.

Figure 58. Davenport pottery cups and saucers. Pink lustre and enamels. Saucer 4⁷/₁₆ ins. :112mm diameter, c.1850.

The cups and saucers in Figure 58 are identical in body, size and shape with those just discussed, but they are decorated in pattern number 863, which is in green and lustre only. The saucers are marked with the impressed anchor and DAVENPORT mark, and were also made in 1852. The cup and saucer in Figure 59 are more difficult to place. They are in porcelain, not pottery, and although the 'Peasant' style decoration is still in pink and copper lustre, green and chocolate brown, it is rather different from 701. The saucer is on the deep side, the cup shape was made by Davenport, but neither piece is marked in any way. On balance, the conclusion is that they were made about 1820-30 but not by Davenport.

Figure 59. Porcelain cup and saucer. Pink lustre and enamels. Saucer 4¹¹/₁₆ ins.:119mm diameter. 1820-30.

Figure 60. Davenport pottery items. Underglaze prints. Jug 3¹/₁₆ ins. :78mm high, c.1850.

Of the miscellaneous items in Figure 60, the cream jug only is un-marked, the others having DAVENPORT printed and an impressed mark decipherable only on the plate, which was made in 1852. The uninteresting sheet pattern of iron crosses is in underglaze blue on the cream jug and plate and in a bluish green on the sugar box. The other sugar box has an underglaze print in the same bluish green of two ladies at a spring in a lakeside landscape. The shapes are clearly recognisable as the same as those in the lustre set.

Davenport Pottery and Porcelain by T.A. Lockett (1972) mentions these wares and comments that 'one is not drawn to admiration by the delicacy of the potting'. We agree, but would add that the gaiety of the lustre decoration is ample compensation.

The general shapes of teapot, sugar box and creamer of the Davenport 1850 set are seen in several others such as that in Figure 52 which has already been discussed. The porcelain set with the monogram FFL (Figure 61), whose owner we tried to trace through the *Dictionary of National Biography,* is also of the same type, but rather smaller. There are differences, of course, in shapes of handles, finials and slop bowl, the last being particularly graceful. The decoration, comprising only monogram and gilt lines, allows the white porcelain to show itself off to advantage. There are six saucers and two plates, but only one saucer has a reasonably

Colour Plate 5. Teapots. Overglaze sepia print on buff ground (35); Davenport with enamel decoration (63).

Figure 61. Porcelain teaset. Gilt decoration. Teapot 3⁷/₁₆ ins.:87mm high, c.1850.

sonorous ring, the remainder being crazed but not cracked.

A part teaset (Figure 62) decorated with an underglaze green sheet pattern of alternate stars and dots shows the same shapes. Saucers are impressed with the intertwined double-D mark of Thomas Dimmock (jun.) and Co. The pattern, which is not particularly compatible with these shapes, occurs also on dinnerware and will be discussed in the appropriate place.

Figure 62. Dimmock pottery teaware. Underglaze green print. Teapot 3¹⁵/₁₆ ins.:100mm high, c.1850.

Figure 63. Davenport pottery teapot. Enamel decoration. 3⅜ins.:86mm high, c.1850.

Returning to Davenport, there is a lovely example of their workmanship in the teapot illustrated in Figure 63. Slight rubbing on the point of the spout reveals a buff-coloured body which has been covered all over, inside and out, with a white slip. This in its turn was given a matt black ground leaving white reserves on which were enamelled fanciful flower sprays in pink, salmon, turquoise, red, blue and yellow. The external shape is simple and elegant, and internally there is an equally elegant hemispherical strainer neatly drilled with nine holes. The mark is DAVENPORT printed in underglaze blue, and a tiny enamelled red mark could be an anchor. Lockett notes several items in this black ware, one of which was made in 1856, but this teapot could well be earlier.

The teaset in Figure 64 is equally lovely, but is marked only with the pattern number 2 over 28, as a fraction with a line between. This occurs on every piece, but is of no help in suggesting a manufacturer. The pieces have good shapes, are well potted in a fine white china with a little moulding on the plates. The decoration is many different flower sprays beautifully enamelled in a wide-ranging palette, four on most items, three on the inside and outside of the cups. The glaze is smooth and lustrous, and has not crazed so that all flatware rings well. The shape suggests a date about 1845, but it might be later. This is a set of undoubted quality that has been well looked after. In fact, it gives the impression of not having been played with, except that one or two pieces are missing.

It may have been noted that a common feature of miniature

Figure 64. Porcelain teaset. Enamel decoration. Teapot 4¹/₁₆ ins.:103mm high, c.1845.

wares is simplicity. No decoration could be simpler than an array of blue dots, as seen on the items in Figure 65. Admittedly there is a small spray in green and cerise, but it tends to be hidden at the bottom of the cup or underneath it in the middle of the saucer. The shapes too are simple but acceptable, and potting and finish are good. There are no marks, but this set also was probably made about the middle of the century.

Figure 65. Porcelain teaset. Blue enamel decoration. Teapot 3¹³/₁₆ ins.:100mm high, mid-19th century.

Figure 66. Porcelain teaset. Green enamel decoration. Teapot 5³/₁₆ ins.:132mm high, mid-19th century.

More obviously mid-Victorian, but not ostentatiously so, is the fluted set with rather elongated teapot and sugar box, both standing on feet (Figure 66). This is decorated only in green, with dots and a few lines. It also is well potted in bone china, like the previous set, and is equally well finished. It matches perfectly one's idealised picture of a demure Victorian Miss.

Figure 67. Porcelain teaset. Enamel decoration. Teapot 3⁷/₁₆ ins.:87mm high, mid-19th century.

The set in Figure 67 has floral enamelled decoration comprising the ubiquitous pink rose alternating with an unidentified blue flower, both with ample foliage. There is much moulding, on the edges of all items as well as finials, teapot spout and sugar box handles. It is not obtrusive but is crisp and evidence of good potting. Compared with some of its mid-century contemporaries, its shapes are restrained and its appearance is pleasing. Most pieces are marked with a pencilled 17 overglaze, but three saucers have No. 18 in a flowing script and the teapot 117 and two small circles joined by a straight line, like a tiny dumb-bell. The round shape of teapot and sugar box has also been seen in the two previous sets.

Some miscellaneous wares from this period are of interest as much for their marks as for any other reason. The cup, saucer and plate in Figure 68 have a print and border of a floral subject in a dull bluish green, but plate and saucer have a printed mark of 'Broadhurst and Green, Bouquet' in a circle surrounding an anchor. The saucer also has an impressed anchor. This firm was active 1845-52, but its products, judged by this example, were

Figure 68. Broadhurst and Green pottery items. Underglaze green print. Plate 5¼ins.:134mm diameter, c.1850.

uninspired. The cup and saucer in Figure 69 are printed in brown with a scene showing two young children playing with a large ferocious-looking dog without supervision. The mesh border includes three vignettes of animals, and the saucer has a large printed cartouche mark with the word 'Infancy' on a shield and the initials B. & S. These initials could apply to several manufacturers. The most likely seems to be Barker and Son, c.1850-60. The blue-printed plate in Figure 70 with the scene of girl and dog in a landscape and a feather border has the impressed mark of STONE-WARE in a semi-circle round B. & T. Assigning a manufacturer, such as Barker and Till, c.1846-50, would be no better than a guess. However, the plate is well printed in a rich blue.

Figure 69. Pottery cup and saucer. Underglaze brown print 'Infancy'. Saucer 4⅞ins.:123mm diameter. Probably Barker and Son 1850-60.

Figure 70. Pottery plate. Blue underglaze print, 4¾ins.:121mm diameter. Probably Barker and Till 1845-50.

Figure 71. Pottery cup and saucer. Underglaze black print. Saucer 4^{11}/$_{16}$ins.:119mm diameter. 1840-45. Probably Swansea.

The cup and saucer in Figure 71 are worth noting if only for their patterns printed in underglaze black. That on the saucer is of a girl seated on a stool in a garden doing her sewing with her book cast on one side and her doll in a wicker basket beside her. The same pattern occurs on one side of the cup, the other having a scene of a girl and boy sitting on the ground in a garden, the girl holding and admiring the boy's boat, with her doll cast on one side. There is an impressed mark on the saucer that could be a small D, and the shapes resemble those on Plate LXXII of *The Pottery and Porcelain of Swansea and Nantgarw* by E. Morton Nance. The cup and saucer may therefore be of Swansea origin, and if so, would be from about 1840 or a little later.

The characteristic and well-engraved dress of the sewing girl on the saucer raises the question of the advisability of dating miniature pieces on the style of costume they display. It may be perfectly legitimate, but it should be remembered that fond Mamas and Aunts, who would purchase sets, might be more attracted by styles of a previous generation. Furthermore, a potter might not be too anxious to try to be contemporary with a pattern that might have to last for several years.

We were in two minds whether to include the pieces illustrated in Figure 72, because the decoration is somewhat crudely commercial and the sizes are perhaps large for miniature wares. The items are resonantly potted in porcelain decorated lightly with underglaze black prints, with much overglaze enamel in many colours, often thickly and crudely applied. The gilding is neat and not brassy, and an unusual feature is a silver lustre that has an apricot colour when not reflecting. The scenes, more fanciful than true to life, include (1) Market Day, Wales (2) A Bidding in Wales (3) Welsh Costumes (4) Welsh Peasantry (5) A Wedding in Wales (6) Sabbath Day in Wales (7) Returning from the Wedding. There is no mark, and dating is difficult, but perhaps 1860-70 or even later.

Figure 72. Porcelain teaware. Underglaze black print and enamels. Teapot 4⁹/₁₆ ins.:116mm high. 1860-70.

It is pleasant to be able to turn to three bone china teasets fully authenticated as to maker and date. They are by Minton, the first (Figure 73) being well potted with moulding outlined and accentuated with green enamel lines. The other decoration is of flower sprays painted overglaze, a pink rose and foliage being common features with many other flowers, a few in each spray. The whole effect is dainty and pleasing. All pieces are marked with the pattern number 7970 pencilled in green, the plate has an impressed M, and most have Minton date mark for 1856, Q. Continuance of the round shape is worth noting, as well as the pineapple finials.

Figure 73. Minton porcelain teaset. Enamel decoration. Teapot 3⅝ins.:92mm high. 1856.

Figure 74. Minton porcelain teaset. Enamel decoration. Teapot 4¹/₁₆ins.:103mm high. 1861-67.

Colour Plate 6. Ewers and basins. Top shelf: flower encrusted, probably Coalport (199); middle and bottom shelves: left, Spode 1970s (205); centre, Spode 1820s; right, maker unknown (200).

Another charming Minton set (Figure 74) is also decorated with flower sprays and blue lines outlining the moulding. Although all the larger sprays incorporate one pink rose, they are all different in makeup or colouring, a feature that is not immediately apparent, and they are excellently painted. The round shape persists, but otherwise this set differs in shapes from the previous one. All handles are bifurcated at the top, and it is worth noting that this is the earliest set we know with a small slop bowl. The pattern number 8533 is pencilled in green on each piece, and all flatware items are impressed MINTON. There are various impressed date marks, for 1861 and 1866 on the two plates, and for 1867 on the four saucers. It would seem that one plate was kept in store for several years before being decorated.

A plate and four cups and saucers only survive of a set (Figure 75) potted in the same bone china as that just described and with similar shapes. They are decorated with the well-known 'Roses, Pansies and Forget-me-nots' pattern, recorded on one cup and saucer as number 9183. The edges and moulding are outlined in maroon. MINTON is impressed on all flatware items, together with date symbols for 1863 on three saucers and for 1864 on one saucer and the plate.

Figure 75. Minton teaware. Enamel decoration. Saucer 4¾ins.:120mm across, c.1865.

During these middle years of the nineteenth century, commercial interests and the Industrial Revolution tended to restrict individuality, but even so, several makers produced well-potted items in pottery or porcelain, often with excellently painted decoration or with transfer prints appropriate for children's use. Admittedly quality was variable, some items being definitely poor, but many had points of commendation and some could be described as of excellent quality. Simplicity of shapes and decoration was apparent throughout apart from a spell when the shapes of teapots and their handles became flamboyant.

(iii) Later Period, 1865-1900

Figure 76 shows two saucers and one cup with a print of three ladies at a tea table with the inscription 'Ladies all I pray make free, and tell me how you like your tea'. One saucer, printed in green, is marked W.C. & Co., and was made by Wood, Challinor and Co., Well Street Pottery, Tunstall 1860-64; the cup and the other saucer are printed in black, the saucer with the mark F. & C., made by Ford and Challinor, Lion Works, Sandyford, Tunstall, 1865-90. The items then were made in the middle 1860s and Mr. Challinor in moving from Well Street to Lion Works must have taken an engraved copper plate with him, for the two saucers have identical prints. These items are not of good quality.

Figure 76. Pottery cup and two saucers. Underglaze prints. Saucer 4⅞ins.:124mm across, c.1865.

Colour Plate 7. Modern Pieces. Wedgwood Children's Story Plate 1979 'The Golden Goose'; Spode commemorative cup and saucer, 1981 (90); Worcester reproduction teapot (88); Spode watering can (205).

72

The following set (Figure 77) is a bit of an anachronism. The saucers have an impressed mark of John Carr and Sons in an oval surrounding an anchor, but there is no stag's head. The set was made in about 1870, but at this late date it still has deep saucers with no well, and a largish slop bowl. The potting is rather coarse, the print in green is less than interesting, but it has been well transferred; it shows a woman with a parasol, a child and a dog under a tree with a mansion by a river in the background. The border is flower sprays with scrolls and honeycomb, and the bluish glaze has crazed, leading to much staining. It seems that children's teasets were something of a speciality of this firm, working in the Low Lights Pottery, North Shields, Northumberland.

Figure 77. John Carr pottery teaset. Underglaze green print. Teapot 3¹/₁₆ ins.:78mm high, c.1870.

Figure 78. Pottery teapot. Underglaze green print. 2¹⁵/₁₆ ins. :75mm high. Probably John Carr, c.1870.

The teapot in Figure 78, while not identical with that in the previous set, has the same general shape and its handle, spout and finial are identical. The green print has a mixture of oriental and English features, but the pot is not marked. An ascription to John Carr is not unreasonable.

A low point in quality was reached by the set in Figure 79 but we include it because with all its imperfections, it has some individuality. The body is sandy coloured, covered with a brown glaze, except for the insides of teapot and jug. There is much moulding, mostly herringbone and fluting, but the sugar box has trees from a very worn mould. The two sides of the teapot do not tally precisely, and its handle has been marked (incised?) to imitate crabstock. The way the glaze has run indicates that various items were fired upside down. The cup handles are thick and clumsy, and the finials are no more than finger-rolled pieces of clay. It could have been made at a country pottery or in the Measham area at any time between 1870 and the end of the century. In its day, it would have been one of the cheapest sets available, but its little owner took good care of it.

Figure 79. Pottery teaset. Moulding and brown glaze. Teapot 3⅜ins.:85mm high. 1870-90.

Figure 80. Derby porcelain teaware. Japan pattern. Teapot 3¹/₁₆ ins.:77mm high, 1880-90.

Passing from one extreme to the other, brings us to some fine Derby pieces, decorated with one of their typical Japan patterns (Figure 80). These are much admired and are doubtless beautifully executed, but the authors regard them as being over luscious, particularly in their extensive gilding. However, this does not detract from the excellence of the body, the potting and the finish. These pieces were made by Stevenson and Hancock, the mark, roughly pencilled in red, being a crown, crossed swords and D, with S on one side and H on the other. The date is possibly 1880-90.

The name of Ridgway had been prominent throughout the nineteenth century, and towards its close continued as Ridgways, who made the set in Figure 81. The pottery body has been well formed into interesting shapes, and the saucers have a more or less sonorous ring depending on the extent of crazing. Furthermore, several items are translucent to a powerful light, the sugar bowl in particular having a uniform translucency, indicating uniformity of potting. Teapot, creamer and sugar box are of hexagonal section, cups and slop bowl circular, handles and spout are square. The sheet pattern of a wide variety of small shapes was beautifully engraved and transferred in blue and retains a remarkable crispness. The printed mark shows RIDGWAYS on a torch overlying a bow with STOKE-ON-TRENT alongside, and the diamond registration

Figure 81. Ridgways pottery teaset. Underglaze blue print. Teapot 3¹/₁₆ ins.:78mm high, 1885-90.

mark for 7th January 1882 surmounted by the name of the pattern — CHINTZ. There are also some impressed numbers, clearest on one plate which has 2 over 89. By comparison with other Ridgways sets to be discussed, this is taken to be a date mark for February 1889.

The Chintz pattern occurs in other colours on similar shapes, such as strawberry pink on a teapot and a blackish brown on cups and saucers for a cabaret set. Similarly, the shapes in Figure 81 have been seen with different prints, notably 'Maidenhair' in a variety of colours.

Some lucky children would have learnt the names of several animals from the set in Figure 82. Although well enough made and finished, it is unenterprising except where the curve of the teapot is continued in that of its lid. It is difficult to count the number of separate animals depicted in the transfers, but it is at least three dozen. Saucers and plates are impressed COPELAND in an arc over a crown, and all items have a printed mark of a square with 'COPELAND late' above it, and 'SPODE' across its middle. The date would seem to be about the last decade of the century but no item is marked 'England'. A decision may have been made not to export. This is the earliest set in our collection to have as many as five plates; all the earlier ones have no more than two, not intended for individual use but for bread and butter or cake.

Figure 82. Copeland pottery teaset. Underglaze blue print. Teapot 4¼ins.:107mm high, c.1890.

Figure 83. Pottery teaset. Underglaze brown prints. Teapot 4¼ins.:107mm high, c.1890.

The main features of interest in the set illustrated in Figure 83 are the prints in underglaze brown, which tell the story of Cinderella. There are six of them, variously distributed, and each with its own caption, viz:

'The Fairy appears to Cinderella'
'Cinderella on her way to the Ball'
'The Prince asks Cinderella to Dance'
'The Clock Strikes Twelve'
'The Prince exclaimed "It must be my Princess" '
'Everybody was Pleased when the Prince Married Cinderella'

There are also small prints of a slipper on a cushion, a grass-hopper and two mice, the last at the base of the teapot spout. All scenes are well engraved and transferred, and the creamy colour of the body forms a good background for them. The shapes, potting and finish are of a good standard, and it is noteworthy that the bowl is again large. Each piece has the Registered Number 128955, indicating that the set was made in 1889 or within a few years thereafter.

During the later years of the nineteenth century imports from the Continent and the Orient were increasing, the latter in particular aimed at the bottom end of the market. In consequence, the home trade had to seek to maintain its sales on quality, but the standard of the competition was such that no great effort was needed. We find, then a general levelling of quality, products being acceptable, without being outstanding.

Twentieth Century Wares

This need not detain us long. The authors started life during its very early years, so that many items now being called antiques they regard as being merely antiquated. Trends noted at the end of the previous century continued into this, and many of its miniature wares are unremarkable. There are exceptions of course, mainly among the artist potters, of which more later, but a few examples of excellent teaware are included here, along with some more ordinary items.

Among the latter is a set decorated with Nursery Rhymes (Figure 84) which was, at the beginning of the century, and still is, a popular form of decoration. This set includes 'Jack and Jill', 'Ding Dong Bell', 'See Saw Margery Daw', 'Old Mother Hubbard', and 'Little Bo Peep', in coloured transfers, and also the appropriate rhymes in black transfers; all are overglaze. The pieces were excellently moulded in a good porcelain body with much moulded decoration, and they are well finished. In spite of all its good points, the set gives the impression of ordinariness. Every piece is marked with an overglaze black print of Atlas supporting a globe with CHAPMAN as its equator, ATLAS CHINA STOKE-ON-TRENT above and ENGLAND COPYRIGHT below. The maker is David Chapman and Sons in about 1905.

This set was purchased in its original box, and the picture inside the lid (Figure 85) is worth recording in spite of staining and other

Figure 84. Chapman porcelain teaset. Nursery rhyme transfers. Teapot 4$^{1}/_{16}$ ins.:104mm high, c.1905.

Figure 85. Picture in lid of box for items in Figure 84.

damage, because it shows so well the styles of children's clothes early in the century. The authors can vouch for their accuracy.

A typical traditional Broseley pattern was used to decorate a Wedgwood set, some remaining pieces of which are shown in Figure 86. They are in a rich underglaze blue, and only the plates have the usual Insect border. All items have a printed mark WEDGWOOD ETRURIA ENGLAND and flatware is impressed WEDGWOOD, as well as date letters (where decipherable) for 1915. The only other feature worth noting is that plates and saucers have stilt marks on both faces, showing that these blemishes are not necessarily a sign of age. The set is undistinguished.

Figure 86. Wedgwood pottery teaware. Underglaze blue print. Plate 4¼ins.:108mm diameter, c.1915.

On several occasions we have been offered items like those in Figure 87 as being made by William Ridgway Son and Co. in about 1840. Admittedly some pieces have the Humphrey's Clock mark carrying the initials W.R.S. & Co, but RIDGWAYS appears over it, a firm that started in about 1880, and ENGLAND under it. These items were certainly made in this century, but evidence for dating will be considered in more detail under Dinnerware. The transfers are of 'Scenes from Chas Dickens Old Curiosity Shop', a title

Figure 87. Ridgways pottery teaware. Underglaze blue print. 'Scenes from Dickens'. Teapot 4⅞ins.:124mm high, c.1915.

which appears also in the mark. They are rather poorly printed in underglaze blue, and none of the four has a title. There is some moulding on all items, but it does not lift them above an ordinary level.

All pieces in Figure 88 have a printed green overglaze mark of interlocked W's surrounding 51 with a crown over and ROYAL WORCESTER round. In a larger circle is REPRODUCTION OF

Figure 88. Worcester porcelain reproduction ware. Underglaze blue print. Coffee pot 4¹⁵/₁₆ ins.:126mm high. 1940-50.

EARLY WORCESTER with three circles and date dots below, and finally MADE IN ENGLAND: BONE CHINA, one word centrally on each side, appears in a horizontal position. Three saucers and six cups have eighteen dots in all, and the remainder including teapot lid, ten dots, indicating manufacture in 1950 and 1942 respectively. All pieces are beautifully potted in a body whose greenish colour by transmitted light matches that of early Worcester. The underglaze blue transfer of the Mansfield pattern is an excellent example of engraving and transferring, while the shapes of teapot and coffee pot reflect admirably those of early Worcester full-sized examples. These are the good points, but it must also be recorded that the gold lines are probably superfluous, that tea bowls would have been more likely than cups, and saucers deeper and without wells. Thus, this excellent set has overreached itself, but the shape of the coffee pot is adequate compensation for its drawbacks.

Figure 89. Spode porcelain cabaret set. Underglaze blue prints. Teapot 2³/₁₆ ins.:55mm high. 1955-70.

The delightful cabaret set in Figure 89 was made by Copeland/Spode probably at various times in the 1955-70 period. All marks have the name Spode and some include Copeland also. The tray, 9ins.:229mm in diameter, has also the printed mark

'Gloucester' which is the modern name for an old pattern mentioned in Leonard Whiter's 'Spode'. Here it is reproduced as an underglaze print in a dark blue. The pieces are finely potted in a body that has the whitest translucency of all we have examined. The shapes of teapot, sugar box and creamer resemble those reproduced by Whiter (No. 319 p. 116) from the Spode 1820 Shape Book, there called 'Low Toy'. Truly a set of great charm and beauty!

A similar set was made in polychrome to celebrate the coronation of the present Queen, and a teacup and saucer were produced by Spode for the wedding of the Prince and Princess of Wales in 1981. Although we stated that we were eschewing commemorative ware, we reproduce the cup and saucer here to bring the record right up to date (Figure 90).

Figure 90. Spode porcelain cup and saucer. Coloured transfers and gilding. Commemorative. Saucer 2⅞ins.:62mm diameter. 1981.

General Comments on Teaware

The most reliable guide to dating is a maker's impressed date symbol or number, but there is some lack of precision when one finds different symbols on the various pieces in what appears to be the same set. A maker's mark is also useful, but it may have been used over a long period. Unmarked wares are often more difficult to date in miniature sizes than in normal full-sized ware. Other criteria must then be used.

Products of the eighteenth century are somewhat easier than

most because of their individuality and lack of standardisation. Variations in body, shapes, styles of decoration and finish are well documented, and are useful in assigning a manufacturer and period to an individual item.

With later wares there are some pointers to be used with caution. Underglaze prints in colours other than blue are generally post-1830, whereas rippled glaze (one having, in reflected light the appearance of sand after a shower) often indicates a date pre-1830. Tea bowls without handles persisted into the early years of the nineteenth century, and deep saucers, without wells for the cup, into the 1830-40 period, but deep saucers occur as late as 1870 in one set. The change from the deep to the shallow type was gradual, and some in 1840-60 could be described as deepish or shallowish. Changes taking place towards the end of the nineteenth century include a much smaller basin or slop bowl, the loss of the lid of the sugar box, making it a sugar bowl, and the introduction of plates for individual use, 4 or 6 in number.

Shape of teapot can be a useful guide to date, but its accuracy is not very great because shapes in miniature ware were liable to persist for considerable periods. The globular shapes of eighteenth century pots are well known, and the London shape seemed to persist from about 1815 to 1835. This then became more ornate in handles, spout and moulding, while remaining oval, and finally evolved into a round shape, still ornate, in about 1850. This round shape in a simple non-ornate form persisted through the 1850s and 60s, more particularly in porcelain, after which there is no discernible trend. There seems to be a tendency for miniature ware to be later than the corresponding shapes in full-sized ware, and for pottery to lag behind porcelain.

So far as cups are concerned, Bute shapes are presumed to precede London shapes by a few (ten to twenty) years.

Patterns can be of much help in dating, but they are an uncertain guide in some instances; an obvious example is the Broseley pattern. They will be discussed more fully in Chapter 6. A word of warning has been included indicating the danger of assigning manufacturer on the basis of pattern alone.

A constant feature of miniature tewares is the simplicity of decoration in patterns that are often only used on such wares and which would appeal to children. Similarly shapes are simple except for a brief period in the mid-nineteenth century. Painting on pottery and porcelain in monochrome and polychrome was often of a high standard, particularly polychrome on porcelain. The standards of quality set in the eighteenth century tended to be maintained into the nineteenth century, except that individuality was tempered by the Industrial Revolution. It was inevitable that some inferior work was produced, but surprising that so many manufacturers strove to maintain the standards set by their predecessors. Nevertheless, there seemed to be a dull period as the nineteenth century turned into the twentieth.

Observations on sonority and translucency are discussed in Chapter 6.

Chapter 3
Dinnerware

The demand for porcelain dinnerware in full sizes was met in the latter part of the seventeenth, and much of the eighteenth century by exports from China. The English manufacturers starting about 1750 encountered difficulties in firing items like plates, and only a few pieces of dinnerware are known until later in the century. However, only the well-to-do could afford either the imported or the indigenous product.

In spite of the difficulties, most English porcelain potters tried their hands at some items of dinnerware, and in the middle of the century sauce boats were a popular item, mainly because their size was amenable to firing. A charming example is shown in Figure 91,

Figure 91. Porcelain sauce boat. Moulded and enamelled. 3¼ins.:83mm high at handle. Derby, c.1760.

Figure 92. Sauce boat in Figure 91, end on.

Figure 93. Leeds creamware toy dinner items, c.1775. Sotheby's.

not necessarily a miniature but small enough to be recorded as such. It is slip-moulded in a good white body finished with a friendly, slightly opacified glaze and a few enamelled sprays. The moulding includes shells and a dolphin. Even this small item no more than 3½ inches long could not escape the ravages of the fire, as judged by the distortion shown in Figure 92. It was made at Derby, c.1760.

In considering pottery dinnerware, it must be remembered that the proper use of a dinner set demands many accessories, such as cutlery, chairs, table and space. Anyone who possessed these could well have afforded porcelain. The development of pottery table-wares, then, depended on the evolution of a social class able and willing to purchase and use them, perhaps in the latter part of the eighteenth century. Full-sized dinner services were made by Chelsea, Worcester, Wedgwood, Leeds and doubtless by others, but production was limited until about 1770. Miniature ware would lag behind somewhat, and the earliest items encountered are from c.1775 (Figure 93).

These are in creamware decorated only with moulding, mostly feather-edge, but also on the terminals of the twisted rope handles. It is not clear whether all the pieces were intended to be in the same set, and the candlestick in particular could be an interloper.

A set from about 1800 made by Josiah Wedgwood is in plain creamware without decoration or moulding, (Figure 94). Every piece is impressed Wedgwood and most have a potter's mark such as a heart on all the plates and D or W on the dishes. They are beautifully potted and glazed with a lustrous greenish glaze sensuous to the touch. On a few pieces the glaze has crazed slightly, and on many it is rippled. The colours of body and glaze are fairly uniform over the various pieces. The Wedgwood Museum at Barlaston has similar pieces, reputed to have been made for Darwin children. The two families were friendly and were in fact related; Josiah Wedgwood's daughter Susannah was the mother of Charles Darwin the naturalist. Unfortunately the handles on the tureen illustrated here have been broken off; we decided not to replace them, partly because the correct shape was not known, but mainly because of an aversion to having modern bits masquerading as nearly 200 years old.

Figure 94. Wedgwood creamware dinner set. Tureen 3¼ins.:83mm high, c.1800.

Figure 95. Wedgwood dinner plate. Painted border 3⅛ins.:80mm diameter, c.1815.

Some plates similar in size and shape to those in Figure 94 and equally light in weight are probably a little later. They are decorated with an enamelled feathery border in a brownish grey with two maroon lines, (Figure 95). They are also impressed WEDGWOOD and the potter's mark resembles a Greek letter nu. The date of manufacture is thought to be c.1815.

Thomas Bewick's woodcuts are well known and one of his tailpieces in the *Book of British Birds* shows an old man standing

Figure 96. Pottery dinner set. Underglaze blue prints. Large tureen 3⅜ins.:86mm high, c.1820.

by a gravestone, a boy with a hoop, and buildings in the background. The gravestone is engraved with the text 'Vanitas, Vanitatum, Omnia Vanitas', and the woodcut is doubtless intended to demonstrate 'Crabbed Age and Youth'. The old man, the gravestone and the boy with the hoop are reproduced in the underglaze blue print on the set in Figure 96, which also includes a boy with a kite and buildings different from those on the woodcut. There were two engravings used in decorating the pottery, one with conifers to the right of the buildings on the left, the other with a group of deciduous trees. The quality of the transfer is poorish, and only by comparing several items was it possible to decipher the inscription on the gravestone as 'Sacred to the memory of .....', the last word indecipherable. There is much line engraving but it seems that the transfers were not taken from a woodcut. The reference in Jewitt's *Ceramic Art of Great Britain* (reprint 1971) to Bewick's woodcuts being used by Sewell and Donkin at St. Anthony's Pottery, Tyneside was in respect of overglaze prints.

The shapes of the tureens are typical of the early years of the nineteenth century, but the potting is on the coarse side with many blemishes. The glaze is of fair quality, blue-tinged, rippled and occasionally crazed. A date of about 1820 seems likely, and Benjamin Adams has been suggested as a possible maker. The pattern is usually known as 'Gravestone' but in an American publication it was called 'Benjamin Franklin flying his kite' which seems to be an entirely fanciful attribution.

The shapes of the tureens of the set in Figure 97 are very similar to those just discussed, leading to the conclusion that they both come from the same period. However, the potting, printing and finish of the set now being considered are much superior, many items being light in weight, with well-transferred prints, and a rippled bluish glaze. On three corners of a small tureen the glaze has broken away revealing a biscuit-coloured body with no trace of a print pattern. The good white surface then seems to be due to a white slip on which the transfer was laid. The set is illustrated in Coysh *Blue and White Transfer Ware 1780-1840* (1974, Figure 86) and ascribed by him to John Rogers on the basis of the pattern which was used by this potter on full-sized ware. This ascription is accepted with only slight hesitation, remembering the 'Cottage' pattern and its border shared by Minton and one of the Godwins

Figure 97. Pottery dinner set. Underglaze blue prints. Large tureen 3¹³/₁₆ins.:97mm high. Probably Rogers, c.1820-30.

(see page 49). The Rogers' pattern is called 'Monopteros' and is from T. & W. Daniell's *Oriental Scenery and Views in Hindoostan* (Coysh loc. cit.). The miniature set was probably made in the 1820-30 period.

In the sets already considered, the sizes of the plates range from just under 2ins.:50mm for the tiny Monopteros plate to nearly 3½ins.:90mm for a Gravestone item. When plates only are available, size is the only criterion for determining whether they are the relics of a dinner set, and if they fall within the above range, it is assumed that they are. The three items in Figure 98 are of this nature that on the left being decorated with an indefinite underglaze blue print having a prominent Oriental figure shaded by a sun canopy carried by a boy behind him, an Oriental building on

Figure 98. Three pottery plates. Underglaze blue prints. Largest 3ins.:76mm diameter. 1810-20.

91

the left and a European one on the right. The border appears to be flowers and foliage, and there is an indented edge. Potting is reasonable with some kiln blemishes, and the deep shape suggests a soup plate. The bluish glaze is rippled and crazed, but is quite lustrous. The mixture of Oriental and European in the print suggests an early date, as does the rippled glaze, but we would hesitate to put it much before 1820. Coysh and Henrywood (loc. cit.) call this pattern 'Queen of Sheba'.

The other two plates in Figure 98 are both decorated with a typical piece of chinoiserie, having pagoda, trees, river and fence but no bridges or figure. The border appears to be of the 'insect' type. The larger plate is excellently and lightly potted and finished with a bluish lustrous, rippled glaze with some crazing. It is reasonably translucent. The potting of the smaller plate is heavier, and there is extensive crazing. Furthermore, the edge is indented, whereas that on the larger plate is plain. Some doubt arises, therefore, as to whether they originate from the same set, but they both probably come from the 1810-20 period. The rippled glaze on two recently acquired oval dishes confirms this dating and they also show clearly a figure in the doorway of the pagoda. The pattern is ascribed by Coysh and Henrywood (loc. cit.) to Davenport, and

Figure 99. Pottery dinner set. Underglaze blue prints 'English Views'. Large tureen and stand 5⅛ins.:130mm high, c.1830. Probably Minton.

called 'Chinoiserie Bridgeless' by them.

The beautiful set in Figure 99 deserves and has received much study. The shapes are attractive and well potted, some pieces a little on the heavy side. Decoration comprises underglaze blue prints of sixteen different topographical views in England, well engraved and transferred with care. They are neatly fitted round the finials and into the bowls of ladles. Flowers and foliage appear in the border, probably convolvulus and lilies of the valley. Twelve of the patterns are named in a printed cartouche like that in Figure 100, but some items have the wrong title, perhaps because the transferrer could not read. There is no indication of maker's initial or name. The finish is good with a clear glaze, slightly rippled on a few items, but uncrazed.

Figure 100. Typical name cartouche from Figure 99.

The twelve named views are:
- (1) Bysham Monastery (Figure 101)
- (2) Lanercost Priory (Figure 103)
- (3) Donington Park (Figure 105)
- (4) Lechlade Bridge (Figure 107)
- (5) Tewkesbury Church (Figure 109)
- (6) Kenelworth Priory (Figure 111)
- (7) Abbey Mill (Figure 113)
- (8) Corf Castle (Figure 114)
- (9) Embdon Castle (Figure 115)
- (10) Entrance to Blaize Castle (Figure 116)
- (11) de Gaunt Castle (Figure 117)
- (12) St Mary's Dover (Figure 118)

Figure 101. Large tureen from Figure 99 'Bysham Monastery'.

Figure 103. Dish from Figure 99 'Lanercost Priory'.

Figure 105. Dish from Figure 99 'Donington Park'.

Figure 102. 'Bysham Monastery' from Grose The Antiquities of England and Wales *(1773-1787).* Birmingham Public Libraries.

Figure 104. 'Lanercost Priory' from Britton and Brayley The Beauties of England and Wales. *(1800-10)* Birmingham Public Libraries.

Figure 106. 'Donington Park' from Britton and Brayley The Beauties of England and Wales. *(1800-10)* Birmingham Public Libraries.

Figure 107. Inside vegetable dish from Figure 99 'Lechlade Bridge'.

Figure 109. Dish from Figure 99 'Tewkesbury Church'.

Figure 111. Plate from Figure 99 'Kenelworth Priory'.

Figure 108.
'Lechlade' from
Cooke and Cooke
The Thames
(1822). Birmingham
Public Libraries.

LECHLADE.

Figure 110. *'Tewkesbury
Church' from Storer and
Greig* The Antiquarian and
Topographical Cabinet
(1817-19).

TEWKESBURY CHURCH,
GLOCESTERSHIRE.

KENILWORTH PRIORY,
WARWICKSHIRE.

Figure 112. *'Kenilworth Priory' from
Storer and Greig* The Antiquarian
and Topographical Cabinet *(1817-19).*

Both small tureens are labelled 'Corf Castle', a view which appears to be on their lids as illustrated. Similarly, the salad bowl with the name 'Lechlade Bridge' is clearly decorated with 'St. Mary's Dover' and the title 'Embdon Castle' on one vegetable dish is more likely to apply to the view on the lids. The ladles have a small portion of the pattern from the corresponding tureen.

The authors have received much help in tracing the origins of some of these views. 'Bysham Monastery' was found in *The Antiquities of England and Wales* (Grose 1773-1787) (Figure 102), 'Lanercost Priory' and 'Donington Park' in *The Beauties of England and Wales* (Britton and Brayley 1800-1810) (Figures 104 and 106), 'Kenelworth Priory' and 'Tewkesbury Church' in *The Antiquarian and Topographical Cabinet* (Storer and Greig 1817-1819) (Figures 112 and 110) and 'Lechlade Bridge' in *The Thames* (Cooke 1822) (Figure 108). Note that the 1807-1811 edition of *The Antiquarian and Topographical Cabinet* has the spelling 'Kenelworth Priory' as on the pottery plate, but that the same view in the later edition, from which the photograph was taken, is captioned 'Kenilworth'. In addition, 'Lechlade Bridge' does not appear in the 1811 edition of *The Thames* which does contain reasonable approximations to two of the unnamed views.

Figure 113. Dish from Figure 99 'Abbey Mill'.

Figure 114. Lid of small tureen from Figure 99 'Corf Castle'.

Figure 115. Lid of vegetable dish from Figure 99 'Embdon Castle'.

Above left: Figure 116. Plate from Figure 99 'Entrance to Blaize Castle'.

Above right: Figure 117. Plate from Figure 99 'De Gaunt Castle'.

Figure 118. Inside bowl from Figure 99 'St. Mary's Dover'.

'Brandenburg House' (Figure 120) is like the print on the outside of the small tureen (Figure 119) and is not in the 1822 edition and 'Villa at Richmond' (Figure 122) which is in both editions, appears to be the origin of the view on the outside of the salad bowl (Figure 121). Finally, 'St Mary's Dover' has been traced to an engraving by George Cooke from a drawing by L. Clennel in 1814.

Figure 119. Small tureen from Figure 99.

Figure 120. 'Brandenburg House' from Cooke and Cooke The Thames *(1811).* Birmingham Public Libraries.

Figure 121. Outside of bowl from Figure 99.

Figure 122. 'Villa at Richmond' from Cooke and Cooke The Thames *(1811).*
Birmingham Public Libraries.

Two unnamed views remain, one on the lid of the large tureen with windmill and fishermen (Figure 123) the other on the gravy boat (Figure 124). The latter is interesting, because the same view occurs on both sides, but the one is a mirror image of the other, involving two engravings; slight differences can be detected.

It is unlikely that the engraver of the sixteen patterns would have worked from four or more books of prints, one in two editions. A more reasonable assumption is that all sixteen appeared in one pirated publication appearing perhaps in the late 1820s. The earliest date for the pottery set would be about 1830 and its characteristics lend weight to this as being somewhere near the date of manufacture.

A tureen decorated with high temperature colours of underglaze green, dull orange and blue resembles very closely the small tureen with English views in respect of size, shape, finials, handles and moulding on lid, body and stand. The main differences are that the printed stand has a foot rim, absent in the other, and that the lids are not quite interchangeable. Both are shown together in Figure 125, which demonstrates their similarities, strong evidence that

Figure 123. Lid of large tureen from Figure 99.

Figure 124. Gravy boat from Figure 99.

Figure 125.
Comparison of
tureen with high
temperature colours
with small tureen
from Figure 99.

both were made in the same factory. The painted example would be
the earlier by some twenty years, and its quality is up to the level of
the printed item, but it has no mark.

Figure 126 illustrates a gravy boat, dish and two plates identical
in size, shape and moulding with the corresponding items in the
English Views set. They are decorated with an uninteresting
'Seaweed' print in underglaze blue; the gravy boat is unmarked, the
smaller plate is impressed O, the larger P and the dish D and 1.
Probably the most significant mark is $\vee$ on the dish.

Figure 126. Pottery
dinnerware. Under-
glaze blue print.
Same shapes as
items in Figure 99.

The Friends of Blue Club Bulletin No. 12, Spring 1976, reporting on the English Views Set mentions three dishes with Lanercost Priory, two with twentieth century Minton date marks, and one impressed 'Improved Stone China' as on the teaset discussed on page 54. Such a twentieth century dish came into our possession recently; it is impressed MINTONS and has the date mark for 1915. Its pattern is identical with that on the 1830 example; in fact they were both taken from the same engraving, including the border and the mark. The later transfer is if anything crisper, so the copper plate had not been used very much in the intervening eighty-five years. If Minton did not make the 1830 set, it would be difficult to explain how they knew the precise size and shape of dish on which to print in 1915. If they did make it, all the nineteenth century items described must be by them also, and a reason found for the impressed mark on the Seaweed dish. Its resemblance to the Minton date mark for 1852 is tenuous. Constance Eileen King in *The Encyclopaedia of Toys* (1978) illustrates three pieces, and indicates that they were probably made by Stevenson. Verbal suggestions from other sources include Riley and Hackwood, but Minton fits most of the evidence, an attribution that would apply also to the other nineteenth century items with varying degrees of probability.

Although Spode's miniatures were mostly of teaware, he made some dinner sets, notably in Tower pattern, a soup plate from which is illustrated in Figure 127. This has the excellent qualities

Figure 127. Spode pottery dinner plate. 'Tower' pattern in underglaze blue 2¹⁵/₁₆ins.:75mm diameter. 1820-30.

Colour Plate 8. Blue and White Plates. 'Monastery on the Hill' Hackwood (130); 'Bridgeless' (98); 'Tower' Spode (127); 'Monopteros', Rogers (97); 'De Gaunt Castle' (117); 'Gravestone' (96).

Figure 128. Spode drabware items. Dish 3¾ins.:96mm long.

expected from Spode, in respect of potting, printing, colour and glaze, which is slightly rippled but not crazed. It has a printed SPODE mark. Two plates and a dish in drabware decorated only with a gold line (Figure 128) and impressed Spode are similar in body and finish to the corresponding items in teaware. The Tower plate is identical in size and shape with the one drabware soup plate. These Spode items probably come from the 1820-30 period.

The Hackwood family of potters covered two generations in the period 1807 to 1855, and they produced several miniature wares. The earliest include a tureen and plate illustrated in Figure 129. The shape of the tureen is indicative of an early date, as is also the absence of foot rim on the plate but the glaze is only slightly

Figure 129. Hackwood pottery dinnerware. Overglaze puce print. Plate 3⁵/₁₆ins.:84mm diameter. 1820-30.

rippled. The puce print is overglaze, very clear and excellently transferred, probably by bat. Edges are outlined in Indian Red, a colour which is at variance with the puce of the print. The plate is somewhat sonorous, but non-translucent. The date is probably 1820-30, and although there is no mark, the pieces can be ascribed to Hackwood with some certainty.

That certainty is provided by the pieces in Figure 130 which are decorated with an underglaze blue print of a pattern called 'Monastery on the Hill', ('Institution' according to Coysh and Henrywood (loc. cit.)). The items are of good all-round quality, the plates and tureen stand being impressed HACKWOOD. The tureen is identical in size, shape, finials and handles with that in the previous illustration, so establishing its authentication. The ladle is the smallest we have seen. Dating is again hazardous, but it could be c.1830 or a bit later. This would also apply to the standard Willow Pattern plate (Figure 131) which is very well potted and

Figure 130.
Hackwood pottery
dinnerware.
Underglaze blue
print. Larger plate
3⅜ins.:86mm
diameter, c.1830.

Colour Plate 9. Typical dinner set (134).

Figure 131. Hackwood pottery plate. Underglaze blue print. 3⁵/₁₆ins.:84mm diameter, c.1830.

printed, but has much fine crazing. Note that there is only one man on the bridge. All these plates and the dish have foot rims.

The three small items in Figure 132 are all decorated with the same trailing sheet pattern, but each has a different mark. The dish is impressed HACKWOOD, one plate has C. & H. LATE HACKWOOD, and the other HARDING, both impressed. Cockson and Harding succeeded Hackwood in 1856, and were succeeded in their turn by Harding in 1863, so they were made at various times. One of the later firms may have inherited impressed unglazed ware from their predecessors. The dish, one of the plates and the smaller Monastery on the Hill plate are very translucent, probably because they are thin.

Figure 132. Hackwood and successors' pottery dinnerware. Underglaze blue print. Dish 2⅝ins.:66mm long. Various dates.

One soup and a dinner plate, clearly from a miniature dinner service, are decorated in underglaze green with a chinoiserie pattern and a floral border (Figure 133). They are therefore a real hotchpotch, and the best estimate one can make of their date is 1830-40. The scene is of a Chinese-looking boat approaching a landing stage with figures and an elaborate awning, and further Oriental buildings in the background. Although they are well enough potted and finished, their maker was not prepared to acknowledge them with a mark.

Figure 133. Pottery dinnerware. Underglaze green print. 3¾ins.:95mm diameter. 1830-40.

Figure 134. Pottery dinner set. Black underglaze print and enamels. Bowl 2ins.:51mm high. 1830-40.

Colourful decoration in the Chinese style is on the set illustrated in Figure 134, which has a black underglaze outline print filled in overglaze with brown, buff and Indian red, the blue being underglaze. All items have an indented edge with moulding on vegetable dishes, bowl and gravy boat. One of the meat dishes has moulded runways and a well for the gravy. The potting of the set is good and the decoration has been effected with care, but there is much crazing. It was doubtless made to be immediately attractive and this ambition has certainly been fulfilled. Most pieces have 664 pencilled in red, presumably a pattern number, and a few have impressed numbers, but there is no indication of maker. Date is estimated as possibly the mid-1830s.

The pattern including a boy pushing a girl in a wheelbarrow already mentioned on teaware (page 53) also occurs on dinnerware (Figure 135). Three items are in underglaze blue and two in underglaze green, the latter being much crisper than the former. It will be noted that the gravy boat and one dish have a pattern of two girls in a landscape, the remainder having the wheelbarrow transfer. However, all have the same border, and the wheelbarrow is on the other side of the gravy boat, so they are all from the same source. Henrywood (*Art and Antiques Weekly,* 24.8.74) illustrates a plate with the same border but a different central pattern stating 'hat it comes from a Children at Play series, c.1840. It is the same

Figure 135. Pottery dinnerware. Underglaze blue and green prints. Gravy boat 2⁹/₁₆ins.:65mm high at handle, c.1840.

size as the larger plate in Figure 135 and has a similar heavily indented edge, also present on the two dishes. It seems likely that the Children at Play series would include more than three patterns, and that they would all be suitable for miniature ware only. The manufacturer then was aiming specifically at his younger clients with childish subjects, also noticeable in some of the teaware made by the Godwins at about the same time. This wheelbarrow dinnerware is reasonably well potted and finished, but has no indication of maker. The border is particularly dainty.

Henrywood (loc. cit.) also illustrates a plate with the same pattern, the same indented edge and of the same size as that in Figure 136, which also includes a dish and lid, all three pieces in underglaze blue. He indicates that the pattern may be 'Souvenir' by William Ridgway. It has a large central urn with two children on each side, those on the left with a globe and reading a book, while those on the right are in rags with discarded irons at their feet; the border is of scrolls, trellis and flowers. There is much moulding on the dish and its lid, and the white handles add a nice touch. The potting and finish of these items are good, but the print is not clear on the lid; they were probably made in 1830-40.

Figure 136. Pottery dinnerware. Underglaze blue prints. Plate 3¹¹/₁₆ins.:94mm diameter. 1830-40.

Figure 137. Pottery dinnerware. Underglaze blue and green prints. Stand 4³/₁₆ins.:106mm long, c.1840.

Figure 138. Pottery plate. Underglaze green print and enamels. 2¾ins. :70mm diameter, c.1840. Probably Minton.

The tureen, stand and plate in Figure 137 are all decorated with the same pattern and border, the first two in green, the last in blue. Its chief features are two birds and a bunch of apples. They are of reasonably acceptable quality, made in about 1840 by an unknown manufacturer, and they do not call for any special comment.

Under teaware (page 54) we discussed a good quality set with an impressed mark 'Improved Stone China', coming to the conclusion that it could have been by Minton. A somewhat similar plate of dinner size, and having the same mark, is illustrated in Figure 138. The underglaze green print is different from that on the teaware, and the flowers are in blue with a yellow centre, but there is a clear family likeness. It may be more than coincidental that this plate is very similar in size and shape to, although thinner than, the smallest plate in the English Views dinner set (page 92) which also was attributed to Minton. So the purchase of one small plate may have made a significant contribution to resolving a sequence of problems of attribution.

The only British porcelain dinnerware in the authors' possession is illustrated in Figure 139. The more interesting pieces such as tureens and dishes have not survived, but the remaining items have their features. The potting in a clean white bone china is heavy but otherwise neat; plates are ten-sided. Decoration comprises groups of three tiny purple dots, with central sprays in green and cerise, all painted overglaze.

Most pieces have a painted mark 2 over 124 fractionally, sometimes with a line between, but it is of no help in establishing maker. The depressing effect of crazing on sonority when lightly struck is well demonstrated by some items. Simplicity is the keynote and there is an evident resemblance to the teaset with blue dot decoration (page 62) and both could have been made at about the same time.

Figure 139. Porcelain dinnerware. Enamel decoration. Gravy boat 3⁵/₁₆ins.:84mm long, mid-19th century.

Figure 140. Alcock dinner set. Underglaze blue print. Large tureen and stand 4⁹/₁₆ins.:116mm high, c.1850.

There must have been some large nurseries in mid-Victorian times, to allow adequate play space for some of the long dinner sets being produced then — not as long as their full-sized counterparts, but by no means insignificant. Thus, sixty pieces survive of the set in Figure 140, and at least two are missing. There are twelve dinner and twelve pudding plates, perhaps to cater for the large families then in vogue. The shapes of the tureen and vegetable dishes in this case are circular, well designed and potted, but the plates tend to vary in thickness. The blue underglaze transfer is an ethereal scene of Gothic buildings, some trees and a few figures; the wide border is formal but simple. Finials appear to be artichokes, but the intention may have been that they should be pineapples. Apart from sundry impressed letters, the only mark is on the stand for the large tureen, and is an impressed beehive surmounting S. A & Co., a mark used by Samuel Alcock and Co. between 1830 and 1859. One clue to more accurate dating is the handle of the gravy boat, which indicates about 1850.

Another gravy boat with the same sort of handle, but of not very elegant shape (Figure 141) is interesting because of the subject of its blue transfer. It shows a girl in typical Victorian costume with long pantaloons taking a dish of food to a zebra behind a fence. The surroundings are partly English, partly exotic, the border being

Figure 141. Gravy boat. Underglaze blue print. 2¹⁵/₁₆ins.:75mm at handle, c.1850. Possibly J.& M.P. Bell.

leaves and basketwork. The suggestion that it was made to commemorate the opening of the London Zoological Gardens in 1828 is a bit fanciful and early. The mark is a small printed bell, so it could have been made by J. & M. P. Bell of Glasgow in about 1850. Was there some zoological activity in Glasgow at that time?

The set illustrated in Figure 142 was the first antique pottery or porcelain of any size acquired by the authors. It is of course

Figure 142. Dimmock dinner set. Underglaze green print. Large tureen and lid 3¹⁵/₁₆ins.:110mm high, c.1850.

116

miniature and was purchased because we liked it, which is a good, sufficient and overriding reason for buying any such goods. The dealer described it as 'Staffordshire — about 1860', but the only mark was 'Pearlware' impressed on one piece. Trying to find the reasons for his description started our interest in miniature china, which is clearly continuing. The attraction of the set lies partly in its shapes which are well designed and executed, but also in its overall good quality, better than that of the teaset with the same star and dot design in underglaze green (page 60). The pattern fits better on this dinnerware than on the teaset, but it would look out of place on any larger pieces. Two plates recently acquired are clearly from the same set and both have the impressed double D mark of Thomas Dimmock (jun.) and Co. who operated potteries at Shelton and Hanley from 1828 to 1859. The set is probably from c.1850, so the dealer's original description of 'Staffordshire', about 1860 was reasonable. However, as a furniture man he would be the first to admit that it was partly a confession of ignorance.

The longevity of the Broseley pattern has been noted in several examples of teaware, its persistence in mid-Victorian times being shown in the dishes in Figure 143. They call for no special comment except to record them as heavily potted but well finished.

Figure 143. Pottery dishes. Underglaze blue print 'Broseley'. Larger 5^{13}/$_{16}$ins.:148mm long. Mid-19th century.

Colour Plate 10. Children's Plates. 'Paul Pry' (152); 'Tabby' (153); Tyneside ? (150); 'Willie and his rabbit' (175); 'Rover Stand up' (151).

Figure 144. Meigh pottery dinner set. Overglaze blue painted. Large tureen, lid and stand 4¾ins.:120mm high, c.1860.

A set (Figure 144) of which one hundred pieces have survived virtually intact deserves a record of its make up, which is:

One large tureen, lid and stand
Four small tureens, lids and stands
Four vegetable dishes and lids
Eleven rectangular dishes in four sizes
Twelve soup plates
Twenty four dinner plates
Twelve pudding plates
Twelve side plates
Four ladles
Two gravy boats

Missing items would include one rectangular dish and one ladle but probably no more. Does one conclude that it has survived so well because it was too large to be used, even on the night of a children's party? The potting is rather clumsy, and the decoration is no more than blue lines and squiggles painted as borders in overglaze blue, simple but effective and well executed. Glazing is normal but there is much crazing. The combinations of acceptable round shapes and simple decoration makes for a visually attractive set, but its potting renders it less pleasant to handle. Many pieces are impressed OPAQUE PORCELAIN, one word above the other and slightly curved; one item is impressed C. MEIGH AND SON, who was doubtless the manufacturer in about 1860.

Figure 145. Copeland pottery dinner set. Brown underglaze print. Large tureen and lid 3½ins.:88mm high, c.1860.

Figure 146. Copeland pottery dinner set. Underglaze blue print. Large tureen and lid and stand, 4⅛ins.:104mm high.

Two Copeland sets probably from the 1850-70 period (Figures 145 and 146) are attractive for different reasons. The first is smaller than most, the gravy boat being 2½ins.:63mm long, which is still too large for the doll's house. It is decorated only with a printed border in underglaze brown of trellis with a climbing plant, probably convolvulus. Shapes, potting and glaze are acceptable and there is little crazing. All pieces have a printed Copeland mark, and many are impressed with a crown with COPELAND in an arc over. The other set is attractive by reason of the simple elegance of its shapes and decoration, the latter being an underglaze blue border of heart shapes. However, the lids are liable to slip into the tureens, a fault of design rather than of potting. Many pieces have Copeland impressed in an arc over a crown, and there are numerous other impressed marks of obscure meaning. Uncrazed flatware items show good sonority when lightly struck. Dates are very much guesswork, as is the assumption that the brown is earlier than the blue.

It is unusual to be able to date a set almost precisely, but the marks on that illustrated in Figure 147 point to 1871 or a year or two later. Many items have an underglaze green print of 'Fishers', the name of the pattern, over C. E. & M. for Cork, Edge and Malkin, who operated in the period 1860-71. In some instances, the

Figure 147. Cork, Edge and Malkin pottery dinner set. Underglaze green print. Large tureen lid and stand, 5⁵/₁₆ins.:135mm high, c.1872.

C has been removed, or partially erased. The mark on a few pieces is Edge Malkin & Co. impressed in an arc, they being the successors to Cork Edge and Malkin in 1871. Clearly a few items were made by the later firm, but they seem to have inherited an engraved copper plate, with pattern and mark, and some biscuitware from their predecessors. They put it all together in their very early years, trying to modify the printed mark. The potting is heavy, and the rather insignificant underglaze green print is of a boy and girl fishing in a stream, with two cattle in the background. It tends to be overpowered by the heavy border. The round shapes and the acorn finials are worth noting.

The very charming set in Figure 148 has a good measure of information to convey, firstly in its marks. Most pieces have an underglaze black print of RIDGWAYS on a torch overlying a bow and STOKE-ON-TRENT to one side. Many have impressed numerals such as 10 over 87, doubtless indicating October 1887; the only years so marked are 1887 and 1888, which are entirely consistent with the printed mark and the absence of 'ENGLAND'. Therefore it is always worthwhile examining Ridgway's ware for impressed date marks. One plate is impressed with a Staffordshire knot carrying the letters R. S. R., the mark of Ridgway, Sparks and Ridgway, who

Figure 148. Ridgway's pottery dinner set. Underglaze black print and enamels. Large tureen and lid 3 11/16 ins.:94mm high, c.1890.

Figure 149. Ridgway's pottery dinnerware. Underglaze blue print. 'Scenes from Dickens'. Large tureen lid and stand 3³/₁₆ins.:81mm high, c.1915.

were followed by Ridgways in 1879 — an eight-year hangover? For its date, this is a set of good quality in respect of design, shape, potting, decoration and finish. The pattern, named 'Persia', is an underglaze black sheet print of flowers and foliage, filled in with brick red enamel and silver lustre, the latter having an apricot colour by transmitted light. There is also some neat outlining in brick red of handles, finials and moulding, making this an attractive set. Many plates have excellent sonority, and there are several examples of good translucency. In fact, eleven plates of the same size were arranged in order of translucency from opaque to very good (0 to 10) and were weighed individually. For eight of them, translucency clearly depended on the thickness, as represented by weight, but three were less translucent than expected from their weights; these three had the lowest densities, indicating perhaps a lower firing temperature.

Decoration with 'Scenes from Chas Dickens Old Curiosity Shop' discussed under teaware also occurs on dinnerware (Figure 149). Shapes of tureens and their stands are interesting, and potting is fairly good, but some of the transfers are not clear, and finials and handles are sketchy. 'England' is printed on all pieces, and a few have the full Humphrey's Clock mark, with the initials W. R. S. & Co., Ridgways above and England below. The most interesting mark, however, is 6 over 15 impressed on one stand. The set was purchased from a local dealer and the authors have met the lady who sold it. It was given to her new when she was a child in 1925-27, which is excellent confirmation that it was made in about 1915. Impressed figures in fractional form on Ridgway's products can therefore be accepted as date marks, the upper figure probably indicating month, and the lower the last two digits of the year.

Several points arise from the general discussion of dinnerware in this chapter, the first being that there are fewer sets than in teaware. The reason is obscure, but it could be because fewer were made, or because the authors have not seen items that they liked. Sets similar in shape to some of those described above but with different decoration have been noted but they hardly warranted inclusion. Perhaps dinner sets were less popular with children — or with mamas or aunts — than teasets. Similarly, the fact that porcelain is represented by only one example is surprising. Others have been seen but the type of decoration usually applied to porcelain often appears unsuitable for dinnerware.

There does not seem to be a succession of shapes as there is with teapots; oval, round and other shapes are distributed more or less at random in the period under discussion. The only exception is provided by plain rectangular tureens with outward sloping sides and pistol-grip finials, which seem to come from the early years of the nineteenth century. Nevertheless, many shapes are interesting, some are beautiful, and few are dull.

In the absence of marks, identification of a manufacturer may be impossible, or at best difficult involving finding and recognising similar sizes and shapes. The advantage of a large collection is obvious. Dating has often approached guesswork, using the same criteria as were discussed under teaware, such as that underglaze prints in colours other than blue are post c.1830.

Most of the sets are in fact printed, and there is a tendency for the sequence of styles on full-sized ware to be followed, namely: chinoiserie, followed by views from books of foreign travel, and then by native topographical views. This is by no means rigid, but bat prints can usually be assigned to a period before 1830. However, there is no criterion for indicating whether blue painted decoration would be used as late as 1860. Prints are sometimes of childish subjects and frequently suitable only for miniature ware.

Quality is variable, very good in the first half of the nineteenth century, poorer in the second, but there are exceptions in both groups. The decline in quality is not all that noticeable, because there is individual scope for variations in shapes all of which are at least interesting. Nevertheless some of the later prints are uninspired and poorly transferred.

One final point we feel we must mention is that we have seventeen ladles from eight different sets in our possession — a remarkable survival of easily fractured pieces.

Chapter 4
Children's Plates

From about 1820 until very nearly the end of the century many potters made plates with a moulded border, often coloured in overglaze, and bearing a printed scene, instructive, sentimental, moralising, humorous or religious. These have come to be known as children's plates, because they were presumably intended for the amusement or improvement of the younger generation. However, few appear to have been used for meals, and some may have rested on cottage shelves. Quality is average to poor, apart from early examples which are good to excellent, but they are often interesting and provide a peep into some aspects of social history in Victorian times.

Very few examples are marked, and dating in the period 1830-80 is hazardous, but an earlier group is clear cut by reason of its characteristics. The remainder have been grouped according to the type of border.

Early Plates

These early examples are well and lightly potted with crisp moulding and a rippled glaze. The first (Figure 150) has no central pattern, but the moulded border of roses, tulips, other flowers and foliage has been neatly enamelled in pink and copper lustre, yellow and green. The body appears to be pearlware. It was purchased in Northumberland, which, together with its colouring, suggests that it was made in the north-east, possibly about 1820. The two plates in Figure 151 have overglaze black prints from line engravings painted over roughly with green, red and a little yellow. One is 'A present for a good girl' and the other title is 'Rover Stand up'. Both have the same moulded uncoloured border of small flowers and foliage. 'Paul Pry' (Figure 152) was the eponymous character in a

Figure 150. Plate. Moulded border with enamels and lustre, c.1820.

Figure 151. Two plates. Black overglaze prints with enamels. Moulded border. 5⁷/₁₆ins.:138mm diameter, c.1825.

Figure 152. Plate. Black overglaze print, moulded border both with enamels. 5½ins.:140mm diameter. 1825-30.

play first produced in 1825, and one would expect an enterprising potter to produce the plate within five years thereafter. The figure is an overglaze black print filled in carefully with pink, green, blue and yellow. The moulded flowers and foliage are carefully painted in blue, green, red and Indian red. The two plates in Figures 153 and 154 both have rippled glazes but underglaze prints in colours other than blue, indicating probably that they were made c.1830. The well-fed, docile tabby in a dull underglaze green looks like an early trial in this colour. The moulding includes various animals, dog, monkey and fox as well as a chariot and some formal patterns. The creamware body has been covered with a white slip. The demure skipping girl is in black underglaze, the edge having a purple lustre line. The larger mouldings include roses, thistles, daffodils (?) and shamrock.

Figure 153. Plate. Underglaze green print, moulded border. 4⅞ins.: 123mm diameter, c.1830.

Figure 154. Plate. Underglaze black print, moulded border. 4¹⁵/₁₆ins.: 125mm across, c.1830.

Mouldings of Swags and Medallions

The crisp moulding on the 'Robinson Crusoe' plate (Figure 155) is not matched by the poor engraving of the print, the misplaced touches of colour and the poor finish. Nevertheless, Robinson Crusoe was a popular character and he doubtless helped the sale of the plate originally. 'John Gilpin pursued as a Highwayman' (Figure 156) is a better proposition, particularly in the printing of its title, but John Gilpin was another popular character and would

Figure 155. Plate. Underglaze black print, with enamels. Moulded border. 5ins.:127mm across.

Figure 156. Plate. Underglaze brown print with enamels. Moulded border. 5¹³/₁₆ins.:148mm diameter.

probably find his way into many homes. The chinoiserie pattern in Figure 157 has the appearance of being early, but there is no other indication in potting or finish that this is so. Most of the pattern is an overglaze red print with touches of blue, green, yellow and red. Moulding and glaze are good but the potting is on the heavy side.

There is no apparent indication that any of these plates came from the same factory. They are of different sizes and the mouldings vary although they are all of the same standard form.

Figure 157. Plate. Overglaze red print with enamels. Moulded border. 6ins.:153mm diameter.

*Figure 158. Three plates. Underglaze black prints. Moulded
'Daisy' borders. 4¾ins.:120mm diameter.*

Daisy Plates

A rim moulded with two or three rows of daisies set close together
was a popular form of decoration, usually uncoloured. The three in
Figure 158 are well moulded and carry simple underglaze prints in
black of very different subjects. 'The Pet Canary' showing a bird-
cage on a table with a girl to one side is entirely suitable for childish
eyes; more doubtful is 'A Backbiter' of a horse being irritated by an
enormous fly; but 'Priestcraft' in which the priest ogles his
girlfriend in an arbour by moonlight would surely not be on display
in the nursery. These have two rows of daisies, but 'My Bird'
(Figure 159) has three, and again a simple underglaze black print.

There may be some contemporary meaning now lost, in the print
of Figure 160, entitled 'Symptoms of going it in style' the letters,
incidentally, being very well engraved. It includes a teapot masquerading as a steam carriage with two footmen and a distraught
driver. There are two rows of daisies and a rope edge.

Figure 159. Plate. Underglaze black print. Moulded 'Daisy' border. 5½ins.:140mm across.

Figure 160. Plate. Underglaze black print. Moulded 'Daisy' border. 5½ins.:140mm across.

It is known that William Smith and Co., Stafford Pottery, Stockton on Tees issued a series based on the months of the year, of which presumably 'May' (Figure 161) is an example, although there is no maker's mark. Once again the decoration is a black underglaze print with some carelessly applied blue, green and yellow.

A peculiar sense of humour is again evident in Figure 162, entitled 'Pig Race' in which pigs with monkeys as jockeys are

Figure 161. Plate. Underglaze black print with enamels. Moulded 'Daisy' border. 5¾ins.:146mm across.

Figure 162. Plate. Underglaze black print with enamels and lustre edge. Moulded 'Daisy' border. 5¹³/₁₆ins.: 148mm across.

passing the winning post in front of the 'Giberalter Tavern' entirely occupied by monkeys. The print is the ubiquitous black underglaze, with red, blue green and yellow enamels. The daisies have fewer petals and are more widely spaced than most. A rope edge was overpainted with copper lustre.

'Juvenile Companions' is from a well-designed and executed engraving and mercifully the print is left without additional colouring (Figure 163). It shows a boy and a girl in a garden admiring a small animal, and is in a very dark bottle green. The plate is in a good white body, reasonably well potted, and has a sonorous ring; it is an example of better quality.

Apart from the three plates in Figure 158, which are clearly from the same source, there is no indication that any one manufacturer was responsible for more than one example. The output therefore must have been phenomenal.

Bailey and Ball Plates
In 1847 the firm of Bailey and Ball registered a moulded design which is slightly overpowering but easily recognisable. It was made in various sizes, two illustrated here, and decorated with a wide variety of prints. Figure 164 is of a girl with two birds entitled 'The Doves', with a few unobtrusive touches of blue, green, red and yellow. 'Robinson Crusoe and his man Friday' is on a very well potted plate (Figure 165) but the black print has been daubed with thick, flat colours, blue, green, brown and purple, that obscure the print without embellishing it. Was the painting done by an amateur after the plate had left the factory? The answer seems to be 'No', because the two circles of colour that Bailey and Ball always included on the moulding are in the same shade of blue as was used on the print. The scene is of Robinson Crusoe discharging a blunderbuss at a group of birds, with Man Friday cowering in fright; it would have been very acceptable uncoloured.

Painted Moulded Borders
Temperance was a common theme on children's plates, well illustrated in Figure 166. The border is moulded in flowers and foliage, coloured in blue, yellow, brown and olive green, the last much darker than many greens. The clear print in underglaze brown shows a central shield with husband and wife on each side as

Figure 163. Plate. Underglaze dark green print. Moulded 'Daisy' border. 6ins.:152mm across.

Above left: Figure 164. Plate. Underglaze black print with enamels. Moulded border with brown rings. 5⁷/₁₆ins.:138mm across. Bailey and Ball, c.1850.

Above: Figure 165. Plate. Underglaze black print obscured with enamels. Moulded border with blue rings. 7⅛ins.:180mm across. Bailey and Ball, c.1850.

Left: Figure 166. Plate. Underglaze brown print. Moulded border with enamels. 5⅛ins.:130mm diameter.

Figure 167. Plate. Painted overglaze lustre. Moulded border with enamels. 5¹³/₁₆ins.:148mm diameter.

Figure 168. Plate. Underglaze brown print. Moulded border with enamels. 5⁵/₁₆ins.:135mm diameter.

supporters, scrolls above and below, and banners held by the two people. On the top scroll we find 'Firm as an Oak', on the two banners, 'Sobriety brings Domestic Comfort'; on the shield 'Industry Plenty Health Wisdom'; and on the bottom scroll 'Be Thou Faithful unto Death'. Two diminutive children lurk near the bottom of the shield.

The border on the cottage lustre plate in Figure 167 is a mixture of flowers and formal designs dabbed with touches of colour. It is doubtful whether a cottage lustre design should be included as a child's plate, but it is unusual in having two cottages.

The size, shape and moulding of the plate in Figure 168 are identical with those of the Paul Pry plate (Figure 152) and it is equally well potted. The moulding is also very well painted in blue, green and yellow, but the plate is later (ten to fifteen years?) than Paul Pry. The underglaze print is in brown of Saint Andrew supporting a Saint Andrew's Cross. So from the same factory there came two identical plates one with a character from the stage, the other from the Bible.

Few examples of decoration based on nursery rhymes have been encountered, but the two plates in Figure 169 based on Old Mother

Colour Plate 11. Dispensers. Spode watering can (212); Lamp feeder (213); Derby bottle (211).

135

Figure 169. Two plates. Underglaze prints in dark green. Moulded border with enamels. 6⅛ins.:155mm diameter.

Hubbard must have come from a fairly long series judging by the doggerel jingles printed on them. They are: (1) 'She went to the hosiers to buy him some hose, And when she came back he was dressed in his clothes'. (2) 'See the Dame's dog is dead and lost all his powers. As he lies on a bier the Dame strews it with flowers'. The plates are thick but the border of flowers and foliage is well moulded; apart from the green leaves, the painted decoration is no more than dabs of blue and Indian red. The prints are in a dark olive green, and the glaze has bubbled.

Plain Moulded Borders
The two plates in Figure 170 are clearly from a series of four on the Seasons, these being Spring and Winter. Neither is very good, the moulding on one being particularly poor, but the prints are clear in underglaze brown. 'Spring' shows mother, father and daughter sitting under a tree in the country, while 'Winter' is of an old man carrying a bundle of wood in the snow. The moulding is peculiar in that it consists of eleven similar complicated shapes, not very evenly distributed.

Another temperance plate 'The Drunken Mother' (Figure 171) shows a woman leaning tipsily against a wall, her baby dropped to the ground, the bystanders worried and concerned and the

Figure 170. Two plates.
Underglaze brown prints.
Moulded border.
6¼ins.:158mm diameter.

Figure 171. Plate. Underglaze
brown print. Moulded border.
6¼ins.:158mm diameter.

innkeeper nonplussed. The scene is well engraved and printed in brown, but potting and moulding are not very good.

Joseph was a popular Biblical subject on which a series of plates could be based, and items from two such series are illustrated in Figure 172. Neither has much to commend it, particularly the one with the heavy print, but they indicate one type of market the potters were trying to cater for. One is superscribed 'Sacred History of Joseph and his Brethren', with the caption 'Judah resigning himself and Brethren into the hands of Joseph'; the other from the 'History of Joseph' shows 'Joseph presenting his aged father to the King of Egypt'.

Figure 172. Two plates. Black underglaze prints. Moulded borders.
6³/₁₆ins.:157mm and 6⁷/₁₆ins.:163mm in diameter.

Motto Plates

If a plate has only a printed motto in a more or less elaborate scroll, the words are usually described as a saying of Benjamin Franklin. No attempt has been made to ascertain whether this is so in the case of the eight plates described here, but they are recorded for the benefit of others.

Six small plates (Figure 173) moulded with two rows of daisies are printed in black with three different types of surrounding scrolls, on three, two and one plates respectively. They could be a complete set, or one might expect a set to be better balanced with the same number of scrolls of each type. However, the six sayings or mottoes are:-

(1) Better to be alone than in bad company
(2) Frugality is a fortune and industry a good estate
(3) Do justice to virtue, forgive human frailty
(4) When the well is dry they know the worth of water
(5) Not to oversee workmen is to leave them your purse open
(6) Diligence is the mother of good lucke. God gives all things to industry

The last has been seen on a completely different plate with a beehive and a girl.

Figure 173. Six plates. Black underglaze prints. Moulded 'Daisy' borders. 3⁹/₁₆ins.:91mm diameter.

Figure 174. Two plates. Brown underglaze prints. Moulded border. 5⅛ins.:131mm diameter.

A much more elaborate scroll-cartouche is on the two plates in Figure 174 printed in brown and one having 'Example is the best of sermons' the other 'Lying is the vice of a slave'. All eight motto plates are of fair quality.

Above left: Figure 175. Plate. Underglaze black print with enamels. Moulded alphabet border. 5⁷/₁₆ins.:138mm diameter.

Above: Figure 176. Plate. Underglaze dark green print. Moulded alphabet border. 5⁹/₁₆ins.:141mm diameter.

Figure 177. Plate. Underglaze black print with enamels. Printed alphabet. 6¼ins.:158mm diameter.

Alphabet Plates

The Victorian desire to instruct finds more subtle expression in alphabet plates on which the letters of the alphabet are moulded on the border. The print is often of a childish subject as in Figure 175, where 'Willie and his rabbit' shows two boys, two rabbits, a dog, a hutch and a largish house in black with green, brown and red colouring. In fact, this is very nearly a typical child's plate, rather heavy, reasonable moulding, a fair black print lightly but inaccurately coloured, and a mixture of interest and instruction.

In the moulded alphabet on the plate in Figure 176, both the S and the Z are reversed, presumably reducing its instructional value.

It carries a quotation from Burns' 'Cotters Saturday Night':
  'The lisping infant prattling on his knee
  Does a' his weary kiaugh and care beguile'
which may indicate that it was made in Scotland. The print in a greenish grey of the cotter, his wife and their lisping infant is from a poorly-designed engraving, and the potting is heavy.

The last item in this chapter, and probably the latest, is marked and was used by a distant relative as a child in the 1890s. So it can truly be described as a child's plate although it has no moulded border (Figure 177). The mark is the registration diamond for September 1882 and the initials B.P. Co. for Brownhills Pottery Co., Tunstall. It has the alphabet printed on the outside of a square which contains a picture of an adult and a young kangaroo. The print is in black coloured in brown and green, more neatly than most. There is one word in each corner of the square 'Wild Animals The Kangaroo'.

General Comments on Children's Plates
As with many other pottery items, the sheer quantity of production is astonishing. The authors have never seen a reasoned estimate of the production run needed to justify the expense of an engraving, but it could well be several hundred. Forty or so prints are included here, representing at least ten thousand plates, and this is but a small proportion of the total. Where did they all go?

The generally low level of quality indicates that they were made to a price and for a particular market and it is obvious that they appealed to that market in spite of their limitations. This may well be a clue to the continuing interest shown in them, very much akin to that in Victorian flat-back figures, although on a smaller scale.

Some ten of the plates show children in Victorian or earlier costumes which an expert in styles might be able to date. Whether this date would apply also to the manufacture of the plate is doubtful (see page 66) but information on several items might help to establish whether the two dates are linked.

There is an article entitled 'Social History in 19th Century Children's Plates' by Alwyn and Angela Cox in *Collectors' Guide*, December 1979. It illustrates twelve plates, all different from those shown here, and has an interesting text.

Chapter 5

Miscellaneous Items

So far we have considered teaware, dinnerware and children's plates, all very much associated with children, either for their use or as their playthings. There are, however, several other types of miniature ware not primarily associated with children, but which may have come into young hands. They include cradles, ewers and basins, jugs, mugs, taper candlesticks, some products of the artist potters and other pieces. Many of them are interesting, some are beautiful and they all warrant a mention.

Cradles

Two hypotheses have been brought forward as to the purpose for which pottery cradles were used in the late eighteenth and early nineteenth centuries. The more likely is that a newly married couple received a gift of a small cradle containing a little coal and salt, with the hope that they would have children and never be short of heat or food. The other is that a small present was taken to the mother of a new baby using the cradle as a gift wrapping. The ones discussed here are 4ins.:100mm to 5½ins.:140mm long, and were made between c.1770 and c.1810, apart from two which are considerably later. None is marked, and it is virtually impossible to assign a manufacturer, because they were made by several potters in various parts of the country.

The oldest is probably that illustrated in Figure 178, decorated with incised lines and green glaze. The latter has been unevenly applied, allowing the body to be revealed as a pale creamware. It was made in a two-piece mould by press moulding thin bats of clay, and the marks left by the pressing operation are clearly visible inside. When the item was removed from the mould, the ends and base would need to be smoothed over to remove any body squeezed

Figure 178. Cradle. Green glaze on creamware. 4⅜ins.:112mm long, c.1770-80.

Figure 179. Cradle. Yellow glaze on creamware. 4¹/₁₆ins.:103mm long, c.1780-90.

Figure 180. Cradle. Yellow glaze on creamware. 4½ins.:114mm long, c.1780-90.

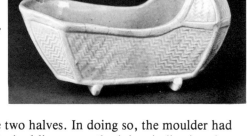

into the gap between the two halves. In doing so, the moulder had to also smooth out the incised lines near the joint, indicating that the decoration was included on the mould, and was not scribed on each piece separately. The rockers are dainty and the item has considerable charm.

The two yellow glaze cradles in Figures 179 and 180 both appear to be creamware bodies, and they have moulded patterns of a basketweave type. The finger marks resulting from pressing into the mould are again apparent, as is the smoothing out of the pattern at the mould joins. The smaller is the more lightly potted, but the larger has a nice flowing shape. There are several defects, such as accretions of kiln dirt, firing and other cracks.

*Figure 181. Cradle.
Green glaze on
creamware.
4⅛ins.:105mm long,
c.1800.*

*Figure 182. Cradle.
High temperature
colours on pearlware.
4⅛ins.:105mm long,
c.1800.*

The similarity in size and shape as well as the moulding in circles
and stipple indicate that the two cradles in Figures 181 and 182
came from the same source. However the rockers are much smaller
on the green glaze example, which appears to have a creamware
body, whereas the other decorated in high temperature colours of
blue, pale brown and yellow, is pearlware. One extraordinary
feature is that on the hood the circles are stretched to ellipses, but
so also are the stipple dots. There is a row of acanthus leaves
moulded at the base of the hood.

Another pair (Figures 183 and 184) are more heavily potted than
the previous examples, particularly the rockers, and they are
sufficiently similar to have come from the same factory. They both
have moulded decoration of incised lines and stipple, rather
different on the two, and one has areas of high temperature

Colour Plate 12. Cradles. 185; 178; 183; 186; 180.

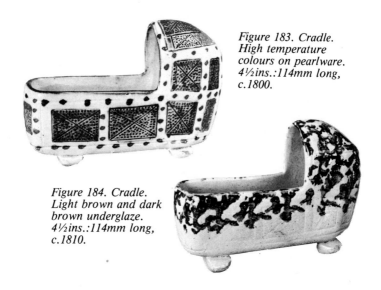

Figure 183. Cradle.
High temperature
colours on pearlware.
4½ins.:114mm long,
c.1800.

Figure 184. Cradle.
Light brown and dark
brown underglaze.
4½ins.:114mm long,
c.1810.

colours, blue, dark green, puce/maroon and light brown. The
other is pale brown all over, with rambling additions of dark
brown.

The green glaze cradle in Figure 185 is well press-moulded with a
sharp basketweave and a rope edge. The even glazing makes it
difficult to determine the type of body, but it seems to be
creamware. The rockers are neat, and each has two imitation nail
or rivet heads. These features and the good shape make this a
particularly attractive example, but they are all worth having.
Marks of the presser's fingers and the smoothing over of moulding
at the ends are features of all eight items.

Two cradles with babies are later. The one without a hood
(Figure 186) has a good basketweave moulding, and the baby's
face, frilly bonnet and coverlet are also well defined. The face is
pink, eyes and eyebrows black, coverlet varying depths of purple
and the outside yellowish brown, all presumably enamel. It has no
rockers but is a well-executed piece.

The other (Figure 187) is of a lower standard of quality. The
potting is careless, the face featureless apart from two black dots
for eyes, but the coverlet is enamelled in blue and red with green
dots. The outside is painted lemon yelow.

It is worth noting that all these cradles are in pottery, and that no porcelain examples have been encountered. The immediate implication is that the nobility and gentry would not use them for presenting their silver spoon or other christening gift, but that the potters were once again aiming at the newly-developed middle classes. The cradles were probably cheap enough to be thrown away, as we do Christmas wrappings, but we are grateful that some at least were kept to remind us of a charming custom when so many infants had no more than a tenuous grip on life.

Figure 185. Cradle. Green glaze on creamware. 5½ins.:140mm long, c.1800.

Figure 186. Cradle with baby. Enamel decoration 4⅝ins.:118mm long, c.1840.

Figure 187. Cradle with baby. Enamel decoration. 4¹/₁₆ins.:103mm long, 1840-50.

*Colour Plate 13. Jugs. Spode (191); 193; Lustre (192); 'Iohn, Kate and Lucy'
(189); Mason (190).*

148

Figure 188. Swansea porcelain jug. Painted with enamels. 2½ins.:63mm high, c.1820. Sotheby's.

Figure 189. Pottery jug. Overglaze brown print with enamels. 2¼ins.: 57mm high, c.1820-30.

Jugs

Except for those included in teasets, miniature jugs were probably made for decoration rather than use. An example is shown in Figure 188, a rare Swansea porcelain jug painted in the manner of William Billingsley. It is 2½ins.:63mm high, has a simple, direct shape and the elegant decoration one expects from Swansea. Its date is about 1820.

On the other hand, a jug of very similar date and shape, made in pottery, (Figure 189) is decorated with a childish subject of two girls and a boy sitting in a garden having a picnic. The title is just 'Iohn, Kate and Lucy' and the two girls are fashionably dressed with large hats and stylish dresses; Lucy carries a sunshade. The print is overglaze in a rich, dark brown, touched in with the same brown, as well as blue, yellow and green. The body is a good white pottery, thrown to produce an acceptable sturdy shape. A date of 1820-30 would perhaps be near the mark.

Mason's Ironstone jugs are among the best-known products of Staffordshire, rivalling perhaps Willow pattern plates. They have been made continuously by Masons and their successors from 1813 until the present day. Two small examples are illustrated in Figure 190 both having the impressed mark 'PATENT IRONSTONE CHINA' in a circle, their dates thus being about 1820. The smaller

Figure 190. Two Mason Ironstone jugs. Underglaze blue and outline prints with enamels. 2⁷/₁₆ins.:62mm and 2⅞ins.:73mm high, c.1820.

has a round section and is decorated fully with dark and light blue, red, apricot and gilding. The handle is a gilded butterfly, and although the piece is well finished, the whole effect is over opulent.

The other jug is traditionally hexagonal, less flamboyantly decorated with an underglaze blue outline print finished with blue, red, green and yellow, It is well potted and finished but the most noteworthy feature of this jug is its translucency to either a strong or a normal light source. Every panel glows almost white, divided from its neighbours by the thicker ribs of the hexagonal shape. But the translucency is not entirely due to changes in thickness, for nowhere is the potting particularly delicate. The other factor, it is thought, is the density of the piece which at 2.37 is higher than that of most pottery and approaches that of porcelain. This could be due to a higher firing temperature or to a more finely ground mix. In either event, there has been greater cohesion accounting for the strength of Ironstone China.

A jug 3¹⁵/₁₆ins.:100mm high (Figure 191) hardly qualifies as a miniature, but it has so many interesting features that it could not be excluded. It has the Spode circular Felspar Porcelain mark, the version introduced about 1825, printed overglaze in black (not purple). This matches the black overglaze outline print which has been very carefully and effectively filled in with a wide range of enamel colours. The decoration includes six Oriental figures and

150

sprays of flowers and foliage, leaving blank areas to show off the whiteness of the felspar porcelain. The pattern, 2644, was probably first introduced in about 1817. By contrast with much of the overglaze colouring already considered, this jug demonstrates the excellent results that can be obtained by a good manufacturer with the outline printing technique. The jug is of standard hexagonal shape, but the wide-sweeping snake handle, that seems to stand off from the body, is worthy of note.

Two lustre jugs in Figure 192 are very difficult to date; they

Figure 192. Two jugs. Lustre decoration. 2⁵/₁₆ins.:59mm and 2⁷/₁₆ins.:62mm high at handles. Mid-19th century.

could have been made at almost any time between 1830 and 1880. One is decorated with copper lustre above and below a broad band of white crumb; it has pink lustre on the inside of the parallel portion and the body appears to be cream. Its quality is not up to that of the other, decorated with a flowing formalised pattern of flowers and foliage in pink and copper lustre on a cream body. It has a very smooth finish with a lustrous glaze. Both have good shapes and are attractive examples.

A previous owner of the jug in Figure 193 had labelled it hopefully 'Coalport 1790-1810', both parts of which we regard with a considerable amount of suspicion. It is a nice enough little bone china jug, well potted and with two good flower sprays painted with a full brush, but Coalport is an unlikely attribution. Date is again difficult, but 1820-30 may be acceptable.

Saltglaze stoneware jugs, like that in Figure 194, are very common except that this one is impressed J. STIFF & SONS, LONDON and also has WALKER'S DAIRY, SLOANE STREET printed in black below the lip. There is an applied moulded figure of two dogs on each side. This is a good sturdy nineteenth century example of a jug made for a specific purpose, its biscuit-coloured body thrown into a satisfying shape, and given a brown dip for the upper parts. Probably about 1870-80.

Figure 193. Porcelain jug. Enamel decoration. 2¼ins.:58mm high. 1820-30.

Figure 194. Stoneware jug. J. Stiff and Son. 3ins.:76mm high. 1870-80.

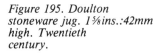

*Figure 195. Doulton
stoneware jug. 1⅝ins.:42mm
high. Twentieth
century.*

The very small item in Figure 195 is similar with applied decoration in white, and the mark DOULTON, LAMBETH, ENGLAND impressed, probably made in this century.

Doulton also made some purely decorative bone china jugs with Christmas themes, three being illustrated in Figure 196. They are decorated with coloured transfers, one of goats in snow, the other two with Father Christmas, reindeer and a motto viz:

'Tobacco and a good coal fire
Are things this season doth require.'
'Let not the hearts, whose sorrow cannot call
This Christmas Merry, slight the festival.'

They have a printed mark indicating that they were made in the first quarter of this century.

Figure 196. Three Doulton porcelain Christmas jugs. Coloured transfer decoration. 2¼ins.:58mm, 2⁹/₁₆ins.:65mm and 2¾ins.:70mm high. 1900-20.

Ewers and Basins

The only miniature bedroom sets known to the authors were made on the Continent in the late nineteenth century, and so would be out of place here. However, small ewers and basins are fairly common, but they were probably decorative rather than useful, particularly those finely painted examples in porcelain.

A pleasant pair in plain creamware is illustrated in Figure 197. The ewer was thrown and its lip formed by pinching on either side. Both items are lightly potted, and finished with a yellowish glaze, that has crazed on the ewer. They are excellent pieces, made probably c.1780, but lack the panache of other creamware items herein.

Figure 197. Creamware ewer and basin. Ewer 2¹/₁₆ins.:52mm high, c.1780.

Spode's outstanding craftmanship is well demonstrated in the pieces of Figure 198. They are very well potted in bone china and beautifully painted in a varied palette with pattern 3710. This was introduced in about 1820, and the other painted mark SPODE would confirm this date. Only the basin is marked, but the ewer clearly belongs to it, and has features that seem to be typical of Spode ewers. These include the turn-down of the lip, and the way in which the handle stands off from the body. These are highly desirable pieces.

Of similar excellence are a ewer and basin (Figure 199) that, although not marked, can be ascribed to Coalport with limited

Figure 198. Spode porcelain ewer and basin. Enamel decoration. Ewer 1¹³/₁₆ins.:46mm high, c.1820.

Figure 199. Porcelain ewer and basin. Flower encrusted and gilding. Ewer 2¹⁵/₁₆ins.:75mm high at handle, c.1820. Probably Coalport.

hesitation. They are well potted in bone china, and the restrained flamboyance of the shape of the ewer is matched by the delicacy of the applied sprays of flowers and foliage, in blue, pink, yellow and green. The gilding is in the same vein. A date of about 1820 seems appropriate.

There are some items that would like to masquerade as Spode or Coalport, but whose origins must still be regarded as doubtful. Such are those in Figures 200 and 201 but their anonymity should

Figure 200. Porcelain ewer and basin. Blue ground, enamels and gilding. Ewer 1⅞ins.:48mm high, c.1830.

not be taken as detracting from their quality, (although it may reduce their monetary value). All are well potted, and the hexagonal pair have very good decoration of blue ground, flowers and gilding. The round shapes are interesting, particularly the eleven undulations round the rim of the basin. These also have good flower sprays and gilding, but the blue ground has suffered at some stage (sunshine? bleach?).

Figure 201. Porcelain ewer and basin. Blue ground, enamels and gilding. Ewer 2¹/₁₆ins.:53mm high at handle, c.1830.

156

Colour Plate 14. Taper candlesticks. Coalport (207); Spode (206); Coalport (208).

Figure 202. Mason Ironstone ewer and basin. Oriental pattern with gilding. Ewer 2¾ins.:70mm high. 1830-40.

A Mason ewer and basin of typical hexagonal form (Figure 202) is well decorated in red, pink and a medium blue with some gilding. Although the pattern is pseudo-Oriental, it is more restrained than many. The pieces are well potted and finished, and have the standard Mason underglaze printed mark in blue with the rounded crown. They may well come from the 1830-40 period.

A heavier Oriental-style pattern in deep blue, red and green (Figure 203) is finished with lustre instead of gilding. This brings it into the category sometimes known as 'gaudy Welsh', but these

Figure 203. Porcelain ewer and basin. Underglaze blue, enamels and lustre. Ewer 3⅛ins.:80mm high. Mid-19th century.

158

Figure 204. Crown Staffordshire ewer and basin. Underglaze blue enamels and gilding. Ewer 1⁵/₁₆ins.:34mm high. 1900-20.

pieces are in a bone china body of good quality, and the decoration although heavy is neat. An assignment can be no more accurate than mid-nineteenth century maker unknown.

Examples from the present century include a very small ewer and basin by Crown Staffordshire (Figure 204) not quite small enough for the doll's house. These are from the earlier years of the century, but the Spode items in Figure 205 are very modern (late 1970s), and are decorated in gold with winged cherubs in various occupations, such as reading and writing. The potting and decoration are of course impeccable, which is also the case with other shapes, such as coffee pot and watering can, having the same type of decoration.

Figure 205. Spode porcelain ewer and basin. Gilding only. Ewer 2⅜ins.:60mm high, c.1970.

Taper Candlesticks

Means for carrying a lighted candle about the house were made in many materials, base and precious metals as well as porcelain and pottery. Although they were often of small size, they were not miniature versions of normally larger articles, but were made for practical use. Whether the magnificent examples illustrated here were ever used could be open to question. The smallest (Figure 206) is marked SPODE painted in red, and is decorated with the popular Imari pattern 967. It has a hole drilled from underneath through to the bottom of the cavity for the candle — purpose unknown. The date of manufacture is about 1815.

Two others dating from about 1820 can be classed as Coalport with a fair degree of certainty although they are both unmarked. The one, Figure 207, exhausts superlatives in respect of its green ground, its flower panels and its gilding. The other (Figure 208) is encrusted almost all over with rows of small similar flowers, a pink row on the outside followed by blue and green, with the same sequence on the three inside rows and the stem, the latter having sagged slightly on firing.

Examples from Flight, Barr and Barr (Figure 209) and from Swansea (Figure 210) are from the same period as the others, and are included to show that many manufacturers made these most attractive miniature items. The sizes of those illustrated range from 2⅝ins.:67mm to 3⅜ins.:85mm in diameter, and they are all excellent examples of the potter's and decorator's skill.

Figure 206. Spode porcelain taper candlestick. Imari decoration and gilding. 2⅝ins.:67mm diameter, c.1815.

Figure 207. Coalport porcelain taper candlestick. Green ground, enamels and gilding. 3⁷/₁₆ins.:87mm diameter, c.1820.

Figure 208. Coalport porcelain taper candlestick. Flower encrusted. 3⁷/₁₆ ins.:87mm diameter, c.1820.

Figure 209. Flight Barr and Barr porcelain taper candlestick. 2¾ins.:70mm diameter. Sotheby's.

Figure 210. Swansea porcelain taper candlestick. 2⅞ins.:73mm diameter. Sotheby's.

Dispensers

A well-to-do home would frequently need receptacles from which to dispense liquids, often scents to counter prevalent smells. In order to be acceptable, the container usually had to be decorative as well as useful, making it attractive to modern eyes.

The Derby example (Figure 211) has a handsome shape with its Imari decoration. Inside the neck is a short length with straight parallel sides, indicating that there should be a stopper. Both bottle and stand are marked with a crown, cross and D roughly painted in red, dating them to about 1820. However, they have different Imari patterns and so are not truly a pair. We understand from the Museum at the Derby factory that the stand is intended for a mustard pot, but we are prepared to let it and the bottle continue to live in sin. They are both heavily potted, and parts are barely translucent.

Another porcelain example (Figure 212) is from the Spode factory, c.1825-30, and is heavily encrusted with raised flowers and foliage, a style not usually associated with Spode. However, the decoration is very similar to that of pattern number 4650, illustrated in Whiter's *Spode*, the bird being a prominent feature in

Figure 211. Derby porcelain bottle and stand. Imari decoration. 4¼ins.:108mm high.

Figure 212. Spode porcelain scent dispenser. Heavily flower encrusted. Handle and spout green. 4ins.:101mm high. 1825-30.

Figure 213. Porcelain lamp feeder. Enamels and gilding 3⁹/₁₆ins.:91mm high, c.1810-20.

Figure 214. Pottery bottle. Black underglaze print, matt black ground and enamels. 3⁵/₁₆ins.:84mm high. 1865-75.

both. The end of the spout is closed and pierced with four holes as in a watering can. The lid matches well, but is not the correct one, which should have small lugs to retain it when the bottle is tipped.

The shape of the bottle in Figure 213, with its firm base, narrow and tall neck and elongated lip, may appear to be exaggerated, but is perfectly practical when its purpose is known. Godden in his book on Ridgway's porcelains reproduces some pages from an original Ridgway pattern book. One of these shows a bottle similar to, but not identical with that shown, and on the original is written 'Lamp Feeder'. An oil container would need a firm base, to prevent it being knocked over, a narrow neck to lessen evaporation and a good lip to fit into the filler hole of the lamp. This well-potted example in porcelain decorated lightly but pleasingly with flowers and gilding is again a piece of pseudo-Coalport, having no mark. It may well be from the 1810-20 period.

The item in Figure 214 was purchased as just another pleasant example of a small container. It is heavily potted in an earthenware base, perhaps with a white slip, and decorated with matt black leaving white reserves of flowers, a bird and a butterfly enamelled over a black outline print. The decoration does not reach the standard of that on the Davenport teapot (Figure 62) but it has been executed neatly. However, careful examination revealed a slip of paper inside on which was printed 'W. Statham Manufacturing Wholesale Perfumer, Lee St., Kingsland Road, London'. W. Statham appears at this address in the 1866 and 1869 editions of the Post Office and London Directories. In 1862 he was in partnership with Yardley (still a well-known name) but he is not recorded in 1876. As the bottle has a parallel portion in its neck for a stopper, it could well have been used in Statham's business, and would then have been made in the 1865-75 period. If he used it as an advertising gimmick, it was quite a charming one.

Creamware
Some further pieces in plain creamware are illustrated in Figure 215, a little pot that could be for mustard, a stand, and two tiny plates with moulded edges. They are all well potted, particularly the stand, and finished in a yellowish glaze. The two plates are a deeper cream than the other items; they are all late eighteenth century.

Figure 215. Miscellaneous creamware. Moulding on plates. Pot 2⁵/₁₆ins. :59mm high. Late 18th century.

Jelly Moulds
Small jelly moulds were intended to produce small jellies for decorating round a larger one. Thus they were miniature but were put to a normal use.

The Wedgwood example in Figure 216 is well moulded in a buff pottery, with half an apple, its stalk and two leaves. It is impressed

*Figure 216.
Wedgwood pottery
jelly mould.
3½ins.:88mm long,
c.1815.*

WEDGWOOD, and dates from about 1815.

The other in the form of an oval, ten-pointed star is in a body that is sufficiently translucent to be porcellanous (Figure 217). Nowhere is the translucency high, and the colour by transmitted light is whitish. It was slip-cast, and would be readily removed from a one piece mould. The irregularity of the mould is interesting, (Figure 218), but one side of the long axis is like the other turned through 180 degrees. It seems that the making of the mould started with a piece that was only half of the finished product. This jelly mould could have been made in about 1800, when experiments with porcelain mixes were being conducted.

*Figure 217. Porcellanous jelly mould.
2¹/₁₆ins.:53mm high, c.1800.*

*Figure 218. Underside view of jelly
mould in Figure 217.*

Miscellaneous Plates

Some plates fit into no category, except that they may be described as decorative. Such is the example in Figure 219, on the large side to be called a miniature, but still just under six inches across. It is in pearlware, with very stylish painted decoration in high temperature colours, blue, dull orange, sage green and dark brown. The edge is wavy and the border painted blue over combed moulding. A good finish is provided by a lustrous, rippled glaze. It is interesting to find three sets of three stilt marks on the underside of the rim. This beautiful plate remains anonymous, but it would have been made in about 1800 or perhaps a bit later.

In the same decorative genre is a plate, impressed WEMYSS, with a lively painting of a goose on grass. The colours include light and dark green, grey, brown and red, the edge having the blue-green hue typical of some products of the Fife Pottery. This item was probably made in about 1890 (Figure 220).

Some small items known as cockle plates are reputed to have been used for serving a helping of shellfish on stalls and elsewhere. The plate in Figure 221, decorated with an underglaze blue print of shells etc., is illustrated by E. Morton Nance and described by him as a cockle plate. It was made in Swansea in about 1840, and is impressed DILLWYN in a curve. The plate in Figure 222 has also been given the same description, but it is considerably later, perhaps c.1880. It is decorated with an underglaze blue printed butterfly.

Since 1971 Wedgwood has issued a series of Children's Story Plates, one every year, the twelfth for 1982 being shown in Figure 223. They are decorated with very colourful transfers, illustrating stories from Hans Andersen and the Brothers Grimm, such as 'The Little Mermaid' 'Rumplestiltskin' and 'The Emperor's New Clothes'. The 1982 example has the 'Lady and the Lion' by the Brothers Grimm. The plates are excellently produced and, as they are specifically made for young collectors, they are not expensive, The authors have acquired a complete set, in the belief that they stand a better chance of being the antiques of the future than many current productions. It is worth recording that, for pottery, they have excellent sonority.

Figure 219. Pearlware plate, decorated with high temperature colours. 5⅞ins.:150mm diameter, c.1800.

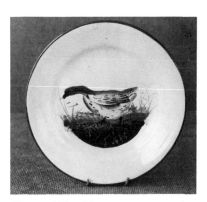

Figure 220. Wemyss pottery plate. Painted underglaze. 4⅝ins.:117mm diameter, c.1890.

Above left: Figure 221. Swansea pottery cockle plate. Underglaze blue print. 4¹/₁₆ins.:103mm diameter, c.1840.

Above right: Figure 222. Pottery cockle plate. Underglaze blue print. 3¼ins.:83mm diameter, c.1880.

Right: Figure 223. Wedgwood pottery Children's Story Plate. Coloured transfer. 6¹/₁₆ins.:154mm diameter, 1982.

Artist Potters

If Doulton may be included among artist potters, then an example from his output sits well amongst those from Martin Brothers, Moorcroft and Ruskin (Figure 224). It depends how one defines an artist potter — perhaps as one who produces individual pieces that are not repeated.

The background on the Doulton flagon, which is heavily potted, is dark grey, brown and occasional touches of beige. The flowers and foliage are applied in white clay, the foliage painted dull green. A description cannot do the piece justice; it is strikingly attractive. The only clear mark on the base is the impressed Doulton/Lambeth mark indicating a date of about 1885.

The Martinware vase is delightfully simple in a cream body decorated only with Edwin Martin's incised pattern, filled in with brown, of two birds in grasses. The incised mark is 'Martin Bros. London and Southall 11 — 1902'.

Miniature pieces of Moorcroft seem to be fairly rare, but the vase illustrated here is so typical that it could be by no-one else. In fact, it has a printed mark 'Moorcroft Made in England' and so is fairly late, say about 1940.

The little bowl has all the appearance of Ruskinware, intermingled pale blue and green on the outside, and yellow and green on the inside with flecks of gold. However, the incised initials W.H.T. are not very clear, and they are not recorded as a mark of W. Howson Taylor, the owner of the Ruskin pottery; a tentative date would be c.1920.

Figure 224. Artist potters. Ruskin, Martin, Doulton and Moorcroft, various decoration and dates (see text). Flagon 2⅝ins.:66mm high.

Popular Bone China

Many of the well-known manufacturers, such as Worcester, Derby and Minton, have continued to make small decorative items, a selection of some popular pieces being shown in Figure 225. Of the two Worcester baskets finished in matt yellow and apricot, the smaller was made in 1903 and the larger in 1912. The Derby mug (one handle) and tyg (three handles) are decorated with flowers, the former with rather sad roses, and the latter with sprays. They are dated 1914 and 1917 respectively. The Mintons pot-pourri has an intertwined handle and the popular 'Roses, Pansies and Forget-me-nots' pattern. Its mark indicates a date of about 1900.

All five items are of good workmanship, and have a measure of individuality, in the sense that their place of manufacture is readily recognised. They are pleasant enough pieces, but of no great artistic merit.

Figure 225. Miscellaneous bone china items. Worcester, Derby and Minton (see text). Mug 1½ins.:38mm high.

Pottery Items

Some pottery items are included here because of their interest, and even perhaps of their rarity. The first is a tinglaze vase (Figure 226) decorated in blue and green with a little gold, and white reserves having brown veining. The authors can only offer a consensus of

Figure 226. Vase, tinglaze with green, blue and brown, some gilding. 2⅞ins.:73mm high. Probably late 18th century.

opinion of those they have consulted. The majority favours the view that the vase is English, late eighteenth century, but Germany has also been suggested, as well as Spain or Portugal, mid-nineteenth century. Opinion as to whether the green is part of the original decoration or was added later is more evenly divided, but there are no obvious signs of a second firing. The shape and potting are good, but there has been considerable chipping of the glaze. The reason for the uncertain identification could be that miniature items in tinglaze are rare, so that there is no body of experience on which to build.

A selection of plain salt-glazed miniature items made by Thomas and John Wedgwood of the Big House, Burslem, is shown in Figure 227. They are lovely examples of the potter's skill, the smallest bowl being only ¾in.:19mm high. Arnold Mountford in *Staffordshire Salt Glazed Stoneware* 1971 records that these and other pieces had been carefully preserved along with some documents, which raises the question as to whether they were made for sale. If so, they would be small girls' cooking aids, but if not, they would be trial or demonstration pieces.

The shape of the item in Figure 228, usually called a butter boat, is common in porcelain, but seems to be rare in pottery. This example is in a light brown body press-moulded with leaves on the outside, and on the base a flower for which the handle forms a

Figure 227. Miscellaneous saltglaze items made by Thomas and John Wedgwood. Smallest bowl ¾in.:19mm high, c.1745. City Museum and Art Gallery, Stoke-on-Trent.

stem. It is thin and light, and probably comes from a period round about 1800, with a considerable margin of error.

The small model of a ginger beer bottle (Figure 229) made in saltglaze stoneware by Doulton in the early years of this century, raises interesting speculations. It is well made and finished, has no decoration and the only added feature is the Doulton impressed mark. It has no obvious use, and is unlikely to have been made as a plaything. If it were an advertising gimmick, some words impressed or printed would be expected. The other possibility is that it was a

Figure 228. Pottery butter boat. Moulded flower and leaves. 3⅛ins.:80mm long, c.1800.

Right: Figure 229. Doulton bottle. 2ins.:50mm high.

171

traveller's sample, which seems to be the most likely. If this is correct, the authors would go so far as to state that it is the only example of a traveller's sample in this book.

General Comments on Miscellaneous Items

The range of products discussed in this chapter illustrate, first, the authors' preferences, and, second, the variety of material that is available. There is a distinct leaning towards pottery, although one might expect porcelain to survive better, being the tougher. The porcelain items, such as ewers and basins, taper candlesticks and dispensers are certainly the more excellent in respect of shape, decoration and finish, but pottery such as cradles, creamware, jelly moulds and artist potters, wins for interest.

The variety of items also carries many suggestions for forming a collection. There is a range of prices from a few tens to a few hundreds of pounds, and a few pieces are even cheaper. If we like a piece we are prepared to accept a limited amount of honest damage, such as a small chip in an insignificant place, or a neat, but still visible, repair. One expects to buy such items at less than full price.

Although some of these miscellaneous items are miniature only in the sense that they are small, and not necessarily too small for normal use, they form a useful foil for pots, tureens, plates, cups, saucers, sugar boxes and gravy boats that form the bulk of miniature wares. We see no incongruity in having them together.

Chapter 6
Conclusions

It is abundantly clear that many, if not most, manufacturers made a variety of miniature items in pottery or porcelain, so that the subject is large, even within the limits set for this book, which can be no more than a somewhat tentative introduction. One private collection cannot be comprehensive, and there is no great quantity in public hands. There are doubtless many interesting pieces in widely scattered private hands, but this would be a difficult source to tap.

However, there are one or two points about the authors' collection that are worth making. It reflects mainly their likes and interests, but it contains also some items that they would regard as uninteresting. These have occasionally served a very useful purpose in comparing their shapes with more highly regarded pieces, but it is then necessary to have both together, so that the comparison may be made with them side by side. But is it worthwhile acquiring insignificant pieces in the hope that they may be useful one day? Another point is that the collection contains some modern pieces that have appealed. They may not be everybody's choice, but the purchase of items from the local store provides an opportunity for ascertaining how one's tastes stand up to the test of time. The authors have had little difficulty in resisting the blandishments of special investment items for collectors.

In making a collection of this type, involving a variety of products, techniques and manufacturers, it is necessary to know something of all these factors. The published literature is of some help, but it is directed more to full-sized than to miniature wares, the latter receiving scant attention. The Norwich Museums Service publication on Lowestoft Blue and White Wares is unusual in providing full information on bodies, shapes, sizes, decoration and finish, but the Norwich Castle Museum has an unusual collection. The authors have endeavoured to plug some of the gaps in knowledge in their descriptions of a variety of items, which may be of help to other collectors. At least it is clear that one can expect to find all kinds of body, shapes, decoration and finish in miniature-sized pieces.

Descriptions would also be expected to contain indications of maker and date. The former is difficult with unmarked examples, and the uncertainty with much ware called Coalport has been stressed. It may sometimes be possible to assign a manufacturer by finding marked and unmarked items that are identical in body, size and shape, but this necessitates having access to both. A warning has been given on the unreliability of assigning a manufacturer because he is known to have used a printed pattern found on an unmarked piece. On the other hand, some patterns, for instance those used at Caughley and Lowestoft, may be very useful in this respect.

Efforts have been made to assign an approximate date to most items using such criteria as seem relevant. The easiest cases of course are those where the maker uses some form of date symbol, either impressed or printed. The former would be made before the item was fired, the latter when it was decorated, and these two could be separated by a few years. So there is some uncertainty even with a date mark. A manufacturer's mark is often helpful in fixing date limits, but some were long lived and therefore not of much assistance; WEDGWOOD is a typical example. Some of the attributes used in dating full-sized ware can be transferred directly to miniature items; they include type of body, glaze, fineness of potting, underglaze or overglaze painting or printing, stipple engraving, rippled glaze etc. These are mostly associated with limitations set by the availability of raw materials and processes. Matters that are more directly under the immediate control of the potter, such as shape, style and fashion, require further discussion, undertaken later in this chapter.

Although it is nice to know the maker and date of individual items, of more importance perhaps is the reaction of the collector to his purchases. Does he really like them and can he say why? Can he recognise their shortcomings? In describing items in their own collection, the authors have tried to indicate their own reactions, recognising that they are subjective and that the reader may not necessarily agree. They also admit that there is great satisfaction is owning a few representative pieces of eighteenth century ware.

The outstanding characteristic of miniature wares is their simplicity, but for the items described herein, this may be no more than a reflection of the authors' taste. Nevertheless, it is difficult to make complicated shapes in small sizes, and having made them, anything other than reasonably simple decoration would be self defeating. A period in the mid-nineteenth century in which teaware shapes became rather ornate has been noted; the full decoration of some items such as the Spode ewer and basin (Figure 198) and scent dispenser (Figure 212) and the Coalport taper candlestick (Figure 208) is not so heavy as to make them unacceptable.

The earliest use of decoration aimed specifically at the younger generation seems to have been on children's plates in the mid-1820s. Adam Buck-style prints were in use at the same time, but they appeared on full-sized as well as on miniature items. On tea and dinnerware the earliest prints for children seem to have been some ten years later, e.g. 'Caledonia' (Figure 47) and 'Wheelbarrow' (Figure 135). It would be wrong to conclude that earlier items were not intended for children. Furthermore, later sets are not necessarily decorated with childish subjects.

A few examples have been noted in both tea and dinnerware of shapes persisting for long periods. There are not enough to decide whether this was common practice, but, if so, it might account for the fact that there seem to be fewer miniature items available than full-sized pieces. Moulds that last a long time are producing ware at a slower rate. There may also be a danger in attempting to date a piece on its shape alone.

The quality of an item can be assessed on the basis of its body, shape, potting, decoration and finish. There is also a rather elusive attribute that we call individuality, present most clearly in eighteenth century wares when trial and experiment led to potters producing items with a markedly individual character. One can quote for instance Whieldon, Wedgwood and Lowestoft. Did this attribute survive the Industrial Revolution, and the standardisation that took place at the beginning of the nineteenth century? Both of these affected mainly the raw materials and manufacturing methods, leaving shapes and decoration to the imagination of the

Colour Plate 15. Artist Potters. Moorcroft, Ruskin, Doulton, Martin Bros. (224).

potter. The shapes of several dinner sets are interesting, and there is imagination in the decoration of some teasets and children's plates. The whole concept and execution of the modern Wedgwood Children's Story Plates, for instance, is imaginative, as are the many patterns designed to appeal to children. So individuality has survived.

On the other hand, there are some pieces with excellent bodies, potting, decoration and finish, but which lack individuality, as for instance the teasets in Figures 64, 73 and 74, and the 'Monopteros' dinner set (Figure 97). This standard of quality is certainly not maintained throughout, but there is usually something to commend, even in items of low quality. Among miscellaneous wares the taper candlesticks and dispensers are certainly excellent, and the products of the artist potters have everything, particularly individuality.

Trends in shape, style or decoration are most noticeable in teaware, possible because this is the largest group. The eighteenth century globular teapot is typical of its period, but the saltglaze potters produced some exciting shapes that follow no trend. In the nineteenth century, the development from the London shape of the 1820s to the rather ornate round shape of the 1850s can be followed readily, a much less ornate type with the same round section persisting into the 1860s. Also worth noting are the disappearance of handleless tea bowls in the early nineteenth century, of deep saucers without wells in about 1840, and of large bowls and sugar box lids towards the end of the century, when individual plates began to appear. There are exceptions to all these trends.

Printing on tea and dinnerware follows a sequence very similar to that on full-sized ware. Stipple engraving was introduced early in the nineteenth century, replacing or supplementing the former line engraving. There are some chinoiserie patterns, followed by views from books of foreign travel and British topographical views, but there are a great many exceptions to this sequence. The introduction of designs specifically for children's items was of course a unique feature.

No trends in the shapes of dinnerware or of children's plates have been observed, and there are insufficient numbers of the various miscellaneous items for any trend to be established.

Miniature pieces will, of necessity, be like full-sized pieces in respect of body and the factors imposed by manufacturing processes, such as slipcasting, glazing etc. It is then legitimate to compare large and small in these attributes, and to draw conclusions such as date or maker of the small item. On the other hand, the miniature will be different from the full-sized in respect of shape, because it will need special moulds. Shapes of bodies, handles, finials and any moulding will be different, in general simpler, thus vitiating any comparison between large and small on details of shape, often very valuable in determining maker. The alternative (used by the authors on several occasions), is to compare small with small, treating miniature products in fact, as being a separate branch of pottery and porcelain. There seems to be a tendency for a particular shape in miniature ware to be later than the same shape in full-sized items and for shapes in pottery to lag behind those in porcelain.

Painted decoration, whether underglaze or enamel, is frequently much simpler on miniature than on full-sized wares. It then becomes difficult to recognise any particular painter or style, but palette could perhaps sometimes be of help. Thus, the use of high temperature colours is a good guide to dating.

Translucency and sonority have been mentioned several times and deserve some discussion. When a porcelain body is fired, the various particles in the biscuit fuse together at their points of contact, giving rise to shrinkage, an increase in strength and in density, and a glass like layer between particles that is more or less continuous. This layer becomes sufficiently continuous to form a path through which light can be transmitted, and to allow a sound vibration to be maintained once started. With a pottery mix, there must be some fusion at points of contact to provide adequate strength but it is less than with porcelain. Consequently shrinkage and density are lower, and the glass-like layer may be sufficiently discontinuous to prevent the transmission of light. However, a greater density than normal as found in some instances indicates more shrinkage and melting and therefore a greater chance for the formation of a continuous light path. Miniature pottery wares frequently have thin sections and this is a common cause of translucency, the transmitted light then having a deep reddish-brown hue. The colour is difficult to explain, but it may arise because the light has to take a devious, convoluted path. However, some pieces with a thicker section transmit almost white light, and these have densities higher than normal. They will clearly be expected to have good strength and sonority, but these attributes can also be affected by the fineness of the particles forming the mix. Thus, the finer the particles the more the points of contact between them, resulting in increased strength and ability to maintain sound vibration.

The effect of crazing of the glaze on sonority has also been mentioned several times. This takes the form of impairing the purity of the tone, reducing its length, or making the sound like that from a cracked plate, although no crack can be detected. The implication is that the crazing extends sufficiently far into the body to impede a sound vibration.

Finally, a word needs to be said on the theory that miniature wares were made as travellers' samples. This theory persists in spite of the facts pointed out by many writers, including Godden and Whiter, that miniatures or 'toys' were made in considerable quantities by several potters and sold through the usual channels.

It is doubtful whether many but the large manufacturers would have employed travellers, and then only in limited numbers. So only a few miniature items would be needed if they were indeed carried by travellers. It is most unlikely that special moulds and perhaps engravings would have been made for a few items, because moulds and engravings are expensive items. Many teasets contain six identical cups and saucers, and dinner sets six plates. If the object was to keep down weight, would the traveller have carried them all? It has been suggested that one item might have been left at each call by the traveller, but then how did they all come together again? As we have said, there is only one item in this book that we believe might have been a traveller's sample.

Why then were miniature items made? The answer is simple: for the amusement of children and sometimes for the delectation of adults. So far as the authors are concerned, they continue to fulfil the latter purpose.

Index